You TWO Can Have A

GREAT

MARRIAGE!

You TWO Can Have A

GREAT

Marriage!

Dr. Walter and Tarsha Gibson

XULON PRESS

Xulon Press
2301 Lucien Way #415
Maitland, FL 32751
407.339.4217
www.xulonpress.com

© 2021 by Dr. Walter and Tarsha Gibson

Printed in the United States of America.

Paperback ISBN-13: 978-1-66280-900-2
Ebook ISBN-13: 978-1-66280-901-9

TABLE OF CONTENTS

BEFORE YOU GET STARTED:

HEY YOU— DON'T TURN THE PAGE YET. YOU DON'T want to skip past this. It'll help you and you will thank us later for the suggestions in this section!

Suggested techniques for getting the maximum BENEFITS from this book:

This book was purposefully designed to work well for an individual as well as for a couple that is married or is considering marriage. Additionally we have intentionally made it useful for groups of couples that want to travel together through a study that will strengthen relationships. The book can be read and exercises completed easily within 2 weeks at a casual pace.

Most couples with the best intentions should be able to complete the study by devoting 1 hour per day every day for 2 weeks to reading independently, working on the questions and then coming together to discuss the content. We believe that although this is the BEST way to complete the book, life happens and it might not work for everyone. With that in mind, we keep the chapters short and thus the book short so that even if you can only discuss the book 2-3 times a week with your spouse, you still will be able to get through the material within 6 to 8 weeks so that you do not lose interest or lose track of principles or challenges that you agree to explore.

Here is what we recommend, although the most important thing is— do something and just start somewhere, even if you cannot commit to this strategy.

1. Prayerfully consider how long you can devote per setting to read and process the content of each chapter. Most people will not need longer than 45 minutes. Again, the chapters are designed to be a quick read (about 10-15 minutes) and take no longer than an additional 15-30 minutes to answer the questions and discuss the content with each other (if you are reading with your mate).

2. Once you determine how long you have available to discuss it, look at a calendar and decide what days in the upcoming weeks (or month) you can commit to time on the book.

3. If you are working with your mate, decide ahead of time what happens if/when the agreed schedule is not adhered to. Discuss whether it is OK for you to hold each other accountable and by what method you will do so. What you DON'T want to happen is for an argument to ensue over a book which is after

all... designed to make your marriage stronger. *THAT* would be an EPIC FAIL!

As mentioned earlier, the material is easily usable for small group studies and the content is even adaptable for intense, accelerated studies at shorter retreats. It is short enough to work through in a matter of weeks or in several group settings throughout a weekend. Even though the read is short, the material allows for discussions to take place and become as in depth as the participants are comfortable with.

Finally, we tried to make the questions and activities ones that would produce opportunities for spouses to engage in conversation and fun activities with one another. The **THINK ABOUT THIS SECTION** is for self-reflection. Some readers may choose to write down their answers, some may choose to discuss their responses with their spouse, but at minimum, we encourage you simply to do as the title states—THINK about it. Be sure that you actually write your answers in the space provided in the **WRITE ABOUT THIS** sections. Really make your time and effort pay off by participating in the activities shown in the **HAVE FUN WITH THIS** sections. We have found that some of the couples that think they are in the most trouble are couples who have simply started taken themselves too seriously and have forgotten how to just let loose, be silly, and have fun!

Also, note that all of the activities and questions are easily adaptable to someone who is working through this book alone. Many times we explicitly tell you how to modify the question or activity, but at other times you may have to think of how you would best adjust it to your current situation. Make the book work for you and know that the results you achieve are directly tied to the effort that is put forth by you.

Our prayer is for the content, challenges and suggested activities to bless your lives and marriages, just as the experiences that we write about have blessed ours. Get ready to be challenged, to learn, and to have fun travelling on this journey with us!

INTRODUCTION

HOW MANY TIMES HAVE YOU ADMIRED THE MARRIAGE of another couple and said, I wish my marriage could be like that? Well, we want you to know that not only can you have a good marriage, but you can have a great marriage. Over the last 25 years, we have come to love each other more and more. Through the tears, lean financial years, struggles, heartbreaks, and disappointments, we can unashamedly and unapologetically say to the world "Yes, we have a great marriage!" And so can you.

There was a time when we felt awkward sharing with people that our marriage was fun and solid because people would respond in critical ways. "Oh, they can't be *that* happy." "It has to be a facade." Well, sorry to all the naysayers, because our marriage is like the old tag line for Campbell's soup— *mmm mmm good!* Please understand that when we refer to our marriage as a great marriage, we are not saying that it is perfect. Over the years, we have come to recognize that marriage is simply two imperfect people who have joined their lives in a covenant agreement and who refuse to break that covenant or give up on each other.

When we talk about marriage, we understand it as a relationship between one man and one woman where husband and wife become one in a lifelong covenant relationship. We believe marriage was instituted by God (Genesis 2:21-25) to be a permanent bond, rooted in love, understanding, respect, sacrifice, joy, peace, and mutual support. The need for friendship, sexual fulfillment, sharing, as well as the fulfillment of the mandate to be fruitful and multiply are all realized within the marital relationship. When marriage is engaged according to God's plan, it models to the world the unity and diversity of the triune God as well as serves as the foundation for a just and solid society. In referencing "the triune God", I mean the Trinity. The word "trinity" is not found in the Bible, but it is a theological term that expresses a truth clearly expressed throughout the Bible. The compact definition of "trinity" is, *God is one in three persons*, which is expressed in the following passages as well as others.

> Therefore, go and make disciples of all the nations, baptizing them in the name of the Father and the Son and the Holy Spirit (Matthew 28:19).

> The grace of the Lord Jesus Christ and the love of God and the fellowship of the Holy Spirit be with you all (2 Corinthians 13:14).

> And I will ask the Father, and he will give you another Advocate, who will never leave you. He is the Holy Spirit, who leads into all truth. The world cannot receive him, because it isn't looking for him and doesn't recognize him. But you know him, because he lives with you now and later will be in you (John 14:16-17).

The Trinity models the ultimate expression of oneness, and the husband and wife are meant to model oneness in the world. Think about each of the phrases from Matthew 19:5-6:

The two are united into one.
They are no longer two but one.
God has joined together.
Let no one split apart.

Just as unity and oneness is a priority in the Trinity, so must it be in marriage. It's important to understand that the unity of the Trinity is not unity simply for its own sake. It's a unity with a mission that seeks to bring others into its way of love. This unity is held together with equality and distinctions. Let's examine this idea a little closer by asking a few questions.

On Equality:

1. *Do you view your spouse as your equal?*

2. *Do you honor your spouse, supporting and valuing them in love? Or is there a sense of control – contempt even – residing in your heart?*

3. *Do you have an unhealthy sense of inferiority?*

4. *Do you encounter your spouse as an equal or do you shrivel away, allowing them to dominate to their and your own detriment?*

5. *Do you both play an equal part in where you're going as a couple?*

On Distinction:

1. *Does your relationship nurture or restrict distinctive strengths in each other?*

2. *Does your marriage nurture or restrict distinctive roles of head and body?*

The way we answer these questions will determine whether we are engaging in marriage according to God's plan and whether our marriage is modeling to the world the unity and diversity of the triune God.

The institution of marriage was designed by God to paint a picture of God, and it must be guarded. Unhealthy marriages are a distortion of God's image in marriage and a misrepresentation of Him. So, like the Trinity, while distinct as persons, husband and wives have equal value, have complementary roles, and are unified by common purpose of mutual honor and affirmation.

Having a great marriage is not automatic. It takes time, patience, commitment, and a willingness to die to yourself daily. Throughout our marriage, we have received counsel from godly couples regarding keys to a lasting marriage. Not only have we received counsel, we have put it into use. What you will read in the following pages is a compilation of stories, ideas, techniques, and proven strategies that if heeded and applied, will take your marriage to a better place of enjoyment and godly fulfillment. But to be clear and completely honest-- it takes work. We have worked hard on our marriage to get it to this point, and if you desire a strong marriage, you will have to put the work in as well. In this book, we hope to show you how.

Recently I was combing through a box of books we had placed in storage. I came across Jim Collin's, *Good to Great*.[1] The book, published in 2001, is a study of 18 of America's enduringly great companies which seeks to answer two questions: Can a good company become a great company? And if so, how?

As I scanned through the book, the notes I had scribbled in the margins brought back memories from a leadership class I took in seminary. Suddenly, I found myself introspectively asking the following:

"Is your life good, or is it great?"
"Are you a good friend, or a great friend?"
"Are you a good father, or a great father?"
"Are you a good pastor, or a great pastor?"
"Are you a good husband, or a great husband?"

Then it hit me. Collin's whole idea centered around key structures and skills that propelled good companies to become great companies. If there are key structures and skills that can propel good companies to become great companies, what are some key structures and skills that can propel a struggling marriage into a good marriage? What are some keys that will propel a good marriage into a great marriage?

One of the distinguishing marks of the companies that went from good to great was the commitment to unearth and face the facts. These companies believed that no matter how dire the facts, as long as they kept the faith, they could overcome any challenge and prevail. The study concluded that this particular mark of great companies was attained

---

[1] Collins, J. C. (2001). Good to great: Why some companies make the leap...and others don't. New York, NY: Harper Business.

by: maintaining a culture that encouraged truth-telling, cultivating respectful debate, and analyzing mistakes without assigning blame.

Many years ago, during an honest discussion, Tarsha told me that I was a better father than husband. Not that I was a terrible husband, I just wasn't a great husband. From that day on, I have sought to never allow that assessment to be the truth in our relationship.

In the pages to follow, we want to share with you some tried and proven strategies that will assist you on your journey to a more fulfilling and enjoyable marriage. The journey will not be easy. Nothing in life of any real value ever is. However, if you make the choice to apply the principles you read in this book, we are convinced that You TWO Can Have a Great Marriage...*too*!

Think About This:

How are you doing so far in your marriage in the area of: love? respect? sacrifice? support?

Write About This:

1. In this section, the author refers to 3 marks of a great company. Do you feel any of these could be used to measure the quality of a marriage?

    _____

    _____

    _____

2. Of these areas- 1) encouraging truth telling, 2) cultivating respectful debate, 3) analyzing mistakes without assigning blame- which one have you had an opportunity to see work well in your relationship?

    _____

    _____

    _____

3. Is there any area shown above that needs a significant amount of attention in your marriage?

    _____

    _____

    _____

Have Fun With This:

Pick an animal, a fruit, a movie title, an advertising slogan, or the title of a board/card game that can describe your marriage. Explain your choice.

_____

_____

_____

_____

_____

Remedial Courses are not Punishment

MANY COLLEGES REQUIRE STUDENTS TO TAKE REMEDIAL classes. When I entered college and even now almost 3 decades later as I listen to students entering colleges, remedial classes can have a very negative stigma attached. "Special ed" classes in middle school and high school were not classes that students wanted to be associated with and for many of the same reasons, college students did not want others to know that they would have to enroll in remedial classes their first year.

Remedial classes are classes that some students must take in order to build up math, reading, or English skills BEFORE they are allowed to take regular college courses. Remedial courses by definition are designed to help position the student for success in the regular college courses that they will be required to take. These courses are for the student who did not get a firm foundation established when initially exposed to the reading, writing or math content or perhaps the student's school setting did not offer any exposure at all to the skills necessary for the particular math, reading or writing course that is coming up for the student. In either case, the need is there for these skills to be taught and learned in the remedial classes so that when the required college-level classes are taken, the student is prepared for success.

There is a point in many marriages where the husband, wife or both realize that they are facing challenges or even just everyday situations for which they did not adequately receive the training necessary to succeed. Perhaps like some of the students mentioned above, it was because they were never exposed to couples, books or conferences that presented teachings on the particular challenge at hand, or maybe it was just simply that when the teaching was offered, the concepts were not effectively grasped. Regardless of the reason, couples need to recognize that if additional teaching needs to take place in the area of intimacy, finances, communication, setting priorities or all of the above, the time for the remedial course is NOW whenever NOW is, whether it is 2 months into a marriage or 20 years into it.

We were at least 10 years into our marriage before we realized we had a very unhealthy relationship with money. We did not understand how it worked and in particular how it should work for us. We paid on bills, made more bills and adopted and settled into the mindset that we could not afford to save. We were more than 15 years into our marriage before I realized that the opinions we had were quite different in regards to how much we should give to our children as they were transitioning from adolescence into young adult life. When our oldest son went off to college, I could not understand why he should be receiving what was essentially a parental stipend to be used for spring break trips and clothing for fraternity events. Afterall, I was the poster child for struggling college students and who was I to deprive my children of the same "opportunity" to be on that poster?

We were over 20 years into the marriage before one of us made the statement, " I am realizing that we have different expectations when it comes to sex" (the BIG reveal on who said that is in the chapter on intimacy). Should it really have taken 2 decades for that conclusion to be drawn? At each of these points of discovery we made very conscious choices to do things like: seek out couples who had "been there and done that" and would be willing to share with us, attend conferences that specifically addressed finances, intimacy and/or parenting, or invest in resources like DVDs and books that would help one or both of us in those areas. The point is and always has been (once it penetrated our hard heads) that no matter how far we were into the marriage, we were likely to discover the need for "remedial classes" in an area that was not mastered at the time that it should have been.

When the need for further teaching is needed, don't be ashamed to invest the time and resources into gathering the knowledge. Just like college, it will cost you less to go through the remedial course than to get to the actual course, fail it and have to repeat. We often encounter couples who have trouble because of the husband's lack of involvement in the lives of the children or the husband not assisting with household chores. The majority of the time the issue is traced back to the absence of adequate past examples of males playing these roles. The husband has a couple of choices once it is admitted that he never had the exposure to another male effectively performing the tasks associated with parenting or helping with the cooking and cleaning. He can use the absence of an example as an excuse for his continued ineptness or he can use the absence of exposure to motivate him to gain the necessary knowledge to serve in and thrive in the role to which he has been called.

Unfortunately, all too often, we see that the choice is the former and in many cases that leads to continued frustration in the relationship itself, but even more detrimental, the passing on of unhealthy examples to the precious gifts which will likely follow in daddy's footsteps when they form households of their own.

So, are you facing some circumstances or life stages in which you feel you could use some sharpening of your skill sets? Does your spouse feel there is a need for extra training or the gathering of knowledge by one or both of you from "missed sessions" in an area of your marriage? If you answered YES to either of the last 2 questions, find yourself a remedial course and pat yourself on the back for recognizing the need for it! Remember this remedial course may be in the form of a conference, a book, an online resource or meeting with a couple or professional who has experience in equipping in that area. Whatever form your remedial class takes, embrace it, learn from it and realize that a remedial course is not punishment.

Think About This:

When was the last time you made a monetary or time investment into resources specifically directed toward the growth of your marital relationship? Examples include, but are not limited to: counseling, videos, books, workshops, conferences, and retreats.

Write About This:

1. When we were in school, each class had various units that would be covered throughout the course. Earth science may have covered units like minerals, volcanoes, earthquakes, and astronomy. A

middle school math class may have had units like ratios, percent-ages, fractions and equations. If there was a year-long course on marriage, what are 8 to 10 units that you think should be taught? (they don't have to be listed in any particular order)

_____

_____

_____

_____

_____

_____

_____

Using the following rating system, place a number from 1 to 5 next to each of the units you listed.

1 - I know virtually nothing on that subject.
2 - I have knowledge of this but I don't really apply it or know how to apply it.
3 - I am at a point where I don't think much about this because it is not an area that I struggle in.
4 - This is a strong area for me.
5 - This is a strong area for me and I feel I have enough knowl-edge and/or experience in it, that I could help an individual or a couple who is struggling in that area.

2. For any area that you rated "1" or "2", what are some practical steps you can take to increase your score in that area?

_____

_____

_____

_____

_____

_____

Have Fun With This:

This section referred a lot to academics to make the bigger point that it is OK to admit what you don't know—you just need to do something about it. Just for fun, let's do some thinking while playing games. Plan for some time in the next two days to **play** a game (old school is great to put you in touch with the kid in you!) and/or **watch** a game show that makes you think. If you are completing the study with your spouse, for an added twist, be competitive in who can answer the most questions if you choose to watch a game show. Recommended game shows to **watch**… *Jeopardy, Who Wants to Be a Millionaire, Family Feud, The Newlywed Game, Price is Right, Wheel of Fortune, Are You Smarter Than a Fifth Grader.* You can find old episodes of most of all of these shows on YouTube. Recommended older games to **play**…Scrabble, Tic-tac-toe, Monopoly, Checkers, Dominoes, Bingo, Connect the Dots.

A Magnificent View
of Marriage

The chasm between the biblical view of marriage and the human view is growing wider from generation to generation. We are experiencing a low, casual, take-it-or-leave-it attitude toward marriage that in many instances makes the biblical view seem absurd to most people. A Pew Research article in 2020 cited more than half of Americans saying marriage is important but not essential to leading a fulfilling life. Amanda Barroso writes, "The public places somewhat more importance on being in a committed romantic relationship than being married."[2]

---

[2] Barroso, A. 2020. "More than Half of Americans say Marriage is important but not essential to leading a fulfilling Life." Pew Research Center, Fact Tank News in the Numbers. Posted February 14, 2020. Accessed January 27, 2021. https://www.pewresearch.org/fact-tank/2020/02/14/more-than-half-of-americans-say-marriage-is-important-but-not-essential-to-leading-a-fulfilling-life/

Kate Bolick, author of the 2011 Atlantic cover story, "All the Single Ladies," suggested that fewer millennials are choosing to get married because the social attitude in modern culture deems the institution of marriage as outdated. "It's time to embrace new ideas about romance and family-and acknowledge the end of traditional marriage as society's highest ideal." [3]

Psychology Today's Susan Pease Gadoua wrote in a 2014 opinion piece, "Millennials Are Changing the Rules on Marriage...Is a beta-marriage a good idea or not?"[4] that marriage offers unquestionable benefits, but it's a stale paradigm. "Rather than having only a choice to marry the same old way, or to not marry, let's get a little imaginative and come up with marital options that would be better suited to a variety of people, including a short-term trial union for younger couples, a child-rearing marriage for those who'd like to be nothing more than co-parents, or a socially acceptable live apart arrangement."

I still believe God's view of marriage is the best way, and when we operate from God's view, our marriages can't help but be blessed. Listen to the apostle Paul as he shares God's view and expectations of marriage:

> *Wives, be subject to your own husbands, as to the Lord. 23 For the*
> *husband is the head of the wife, as Christ also is the head of the*
> *church, He Himself being the Savior of the body. 24 But as the*
> *church is subject to Christ, so also the wives ought to be to their*

---

[3] Bolick, K. 2011. "All the Single Ladies." Atlantic. November. Accessed August 15, 2020. www.theatlantic.com/magazine/archive/2011/11/all-the-single-ladies/308654/.

[4] Gadoua, S. P. 2014. "Millennials Are Changing the Rules of Marriage." Psychology Today. Posted August 7,2014. Accessed July 1, 2020. https://www.psychologytoday.com/us/blog/contemplating-divorce/201408/millennials-are-changing-the-rules-marriage

husbands in everything.25 Husbands, love your wives, just as Christ also loved the church and gave Himself up for her, 26 so that He might sanctify her, having cleansed her by the washing of water with the word, 27 that He might present to Himself the church in all her glory, having no spot or wrinkle or any such thing; but that she would be holy and blameless.28 So husbands ought also to love their own wives as their own bodies. He who loves his own wife loves himself; 29 for no one ever hated his own flesh, but nourishes and cherishes it, just as Christ also does the church, 30 because we are members of His body. 31 For this reason a man shall leave his father and mother and shall be joined to his wife, and the two shall become one flesh. 32 This mystery is great; but I am speaking with reference to Christ and the church. 33 Nevertheless, each individual among you also is to love his own wife even as himself, and the wife must see to it that she respects her husband. (Ephesians 5:22-33)

What a magnificent view of marriage!

Sylvia Smith in her article, "5 Facets of the True Meaning of Marriage" [5] suggests the differences that exist in the definition of a good marriage occur from culture to culture, and even within a culture, from person to person. Views and definitions of marriage have also changed significantly over the centuries and decades. She lists five facets of marriage that can help us understand the true meaning of marriage that clearly mirror the magnificent view of marriage espoused by the Apostle Paul:

---

[5] Smith, S. 2020. "5 Facets of the True Meaning of Marriage." Marriage.com. November. Accessed November 5, 2020. www.marriage.com/advice/relationship/ five-facets-of-the-true-meaning-of-marriage/

1. Marriage means being in agreement.
2. Marriage means letting go of your selfishness.
3. The meaning of marriage is to become one.
4. Marriage means shaping a new generation.
5. Marriage means changing, learning, and growing.[6]

Smith concludes her article by affirming that "the true meaning of marriage is to accept the other person and adjust to the various situations that you encounter in marriage to make it really work. The biblical definition of marriage also carries this same important concept."[7]

In light of the words of Paul and Smith's 5 facets, allow me for the remainder of this chapter to help you consider a magnificent view of marriage that is higher, deeper, stronger and more glorious than anything this culture has ever imagined. In order to do so, let's go back to an earlier time in history.

In the first century, many pagan marriages consisted of a man having a wife much younger than himself. He went to other women for the pleasure aspects of marriage, taking on a wife only to have legitimate children. This wife might be 13 or 14 years old, entering an arranged marriage, often against her will and often with a man she had never met. Not much communication, cooperation, or affection could really be expected.

But new life in Christ called for new patterns of marriage. Paul instructed the husband to love his wife and to seek her personal

---

[6] Smith, S. 2020. "5 Facets of the True Meaning of Marriage." Marriage.com. November. Accessed November 5, 2020. www.marriage.com/advice/relationship/five-facets-of-the-true-meaning-of-marriage/

[7] Smith, S. 2020. "5 Facets of the True Meaning of Marriage." Marriage.com. November. Accessed November 5, 2020. www.marriage.com/advice/relationship/five-facets-of-the-true-meaning-of-marriage/

development- a radically new idea in that culture. The wife was to wholeheartedly respond to the love of her husband with commitment and loyalty, not as a slave in the relationship, but as a unique representation of the oneness of marriage. To this end, Paul makes a startling statement in verse 32, *This mystery is great; but I am speaking with reference to Christ and the church.* What does Paul want us to realize as he uses marriage as a metaphor for the relationship between Jesus and the church?

I. Marriage is a shadow of our expected relationship with Jesus Christ.

The gospel message declares that Jesus Christ came all the way from heaven to earth to secure our salvation through His finished work on the cross. When we consider His life, we recognize that everything He did was a part of God's plan to give humanity the way to enjoy a permanent relationship with himself. When we accept Jesus as our Lord and Savior, our relationship with God is sealed by the Holy Spirit. The relationship cannot be undone.

When God designed marriage, He expected it to be an earthly shadow of the permanent, loving, and committed relationship that His covenant children are to have with His Son. This is what Paul describes when he says, *For this reason a man shall leave his father and mother and shall be joined to his wife, and the two shall become one flesh. This mystery is great: but I am speaking with reference to Christ and the church* (Eph. 5:31-32 NASB). Marriage should never be entered under the premise of... "if it doesn't work out how I want it to, I'll cut ties and try it again." When we say "I do", it is a permanent agreement. Marriage should never be engaged under the premise that I will love my spouse as long as he/she makes me happy. No human being has the capacity to make us happy all the time. Marriage serves as a shadow of God's expected relationship between His covenant children and His Son when we love one another whether we are happy or sad. When we love one another through the good and the bad, we display through our marriages the unconditional love that Jesus has for us. From this day forward, pray for the strength and wisdom to ensure that your marriage is a shadow of what a permanent, loving, committed relationship with God the Father through His Son Jesus Christ looks like.

II. Marriage exists to display God's glory.

The concept of covenant is rooted in the bible and can be understood as a binding agreement in which both participants have responsibilities and can expect benefits in return. While some view marriage as a contract or a business deal, the marriage covenant is so much more. It is a metaphor of the permanent union between Jesus Christ and the church. Just as the Father willed Jesus Christ and the church to be one body (1 Cor. 12:12,13), He also willed that the husband and wife be one (Gen.2:24). Paul lets us know that marriage is patterned after Christ's covenant relationship with the church. Therefore, the ultimate purpose of marriage is to put the covenant relationship of Christ and His church on display. The relationship between Christ and the church is a holy thing, and when we operate our marriage according to biblical principles, it displays the holiness of God. That's what "the glory of God" means. It is God's holiness (distinct perfection, greatness, and worth) put on display through the actions of His people. As the Psalmist declares, *The heavens are telling the glory of God* (Psalm 19:1), Christian marriage, when operating according to God's mandates to reflect God's image, reigning in spiritual warfare, and reproducing children in God's likeness also tells the glory of God. When I place Tarsha's needs before my own, I am telling the glory of God. When we are both tired after a long day's work, and Tarsha gets out of bed to fill up my empty water bottle, she is telling the glory of God. When my children live God-honoring lives, they are telling the glory of God. When we give public praise to one another, we are telling the glory of God. When we refuse to let the sun go down on our wrath, we are telling the glory of God. When we pray together, worship together, serve together, and play together, we are telling the glory of God.

From 2006 to early 2020, I (Walter) served as the Senior Pastor of a church in the midwest. During my tenure, Tarsha served faithfully right by my side. I know beyond the shadow of a doubt that I could not have done it without her unwavering, unconditional support. Often, people would lovingly refer to us as the dynamic duo, and they were correct. We prayed together, worshipped together, served together, and unapologetically played together. We wanted to ensure that those God had called us to lead saw who we really were outside the four walls of the church. Whether they saw us in the church or out in public, they would see the same loving, covenant committed couple that we were striving to be. As we look back over that season of life, we are aware of the marriages that God allowed us to have a positive impact on simply by remaining committed to God's view of marriage. While we spent hours counseling couples in our offices, we were constantly reminded that much more of what the couples gleaned from us was caught through observation than taught through sermons and counseling sessions.

When people witness our marriage in operation and admire it, we make it known that our marriage is what it is because of who God is and what He has done in us and through us as we obey His marriage mandates. That is what we must envision for our marriages. Godly marriages must serve as instruments in the earth realm that point to the greatness of our all-wise, all-loving God who created the marriage institution. When we follow His plan for what He created, we will enjoy the fruits of marriage that He promises. That's why marriage exists.

III. Staying married isn't just about staying in love.

Love is an important aspect of marriage. Typically in a free-choice marriage, when asked why they want to get married, the answer is "I love him or her." According to a 2013 Pew Research Center survey, about nine-in-ten Americans (88%) cited love as a very important reason to get married, ahead of making a lifelong commitment (81%) and companionship (76%). Yes, love is important to marriage, but contrary to the words of The Beatles, "All you need is love, love. Love is all you need", I suggest that in order for your marriage to grow stronger and endure, there has to be a commitment beyond staying in love. Why do I suggest this? Well, in my years of counseling couples and talking to divorced men and women, when asked if they still loved the one they divorced, many of them said yes. So, if all we need is love to make marriage work, why are there so many divorces? If marriage is not just about staying in love, then what is it about? Marriage is about keeping a covenant. "Till death do us part," or, "As long as we both shall live" is a sacred covenant promise — the same kind Jesus made with His bride when He died for her.

The key to understanding covenant is to remember it always means being loyal to the other party; it is never simply an agreement to perform some external duty. A marriage covenant consists of death to our single nature, new creation as a couple before God, and a commitment to the vows made.

Do you remember responding to and repeating these words before God and in the presence of the witnesses and guests you invited to your ceremony:

> *Will you, _____, have _____ to be your husband/wife? Will you love him/her, comfort and keep him/her, and forsaking all others remain true to him/her as long as you both shall live?*

> *I, _____, take thee _____, to be my husband/wife, to have and to hold, from this day forward, for better, for worse, for richer, for poorer, in sickness and in health, to love and to cherish, until we are parted by death, and before God and these witnesses I promise to be a faithful and true husband/wife. This is my solemn vow.*

I came across this sometime ago while doing some research on marriage:

> *It is not love alone that keeps us together. In every marriage, love may fade, for a while. The vows matter, because when feelings fade, the vows hold us together long enough for the love to return.*

If we would take these words to heart, the number of divorces would decrease dramatically. Remember, you VOWED. I know the world thinks that if you're not happy, the marriage isn't legitimate. That's why many secular marriage ceremonies are leaving vows out altogether. But if the vow meant, "we'll stay married as long as we're happy", there would be no need for a vow!

The vow is what will hold you together, and God asked you to make that vow. God asked you to commit, because in committing to someone for life, we're also creating a situation where we need to lean on God. When marriage is hard, you need God more. For marriages to improve, you need to emphasize God more, and yourself less. Through the grace of God, you can enjoy a long and loving marriage.

Think About This:

Have you had any opportunities in your marriage to see personal truth in the quote below?

> *It is not love alone that keeps us together. In every marriage, love may fade, for a while. The vows matter, because when feelings fade, the vows hold us together long enough for the love to return.*

Write About This:

1. What words can you think of that describe God's character? Try to think of at least 10.

_____ _____

_____ _____

_____ _____

_____ _____

_____ _____

2. Choose 3 of these descriptive words that you and your spouse reflect in your marital relationship? Explain why you chose each of those 3 words.

   _____

   _____

   _____

   _____

   _____

   _____

   _____

3. What did the two statements below by Paul mean to you when you first got married and what do they mean to you now?

   a. *Wives, be subject to your own husbands, as to the Lord.*

   _____

   _____

   _____

   _____

   _____

b. *Husbands, love your wives as Christ loved the church, and gave Himself up for her.*

_____

_____

_____

_____

_____

_____

4. Is it realistic to expect your spouse to make you happy all the time? Explain your answer.

_____

_____

_____

_____

_____

_____

Have Fun With This:

Look at pictures or video footage from your wedding day. Write down 8-10 words to describe what you were feeling that day.

_____   _____

_____   _____

_____   _____

_____   _____

_____   _____

Are you reading the book alone or do you not have wedding pics or video footage? Use YouTube (or any internet site you choose) to find videos of royal weddings, celebrity weddings or any footage of a wedding ceremony). What are some of the emotions that you see present in those in the video? Try to pay attention to a variety of people in the video...the bride, the groom, parents, officiants, flower girl, just to name a few. Remember—HAVE FUN WITH THIS!

SPECIAL DELIVERY

A WEALTHY WOMAN WHO WAS TRAVELING OVERSEAS saw a bracelet she thought was irresistible, so she sent her husband this wired message: "Have found wonderful bracelet. Price $75,000. May I buy it?" Her husband promptly wired back this response: "No, price too high." But the cable operator omitted the comma, so the woman received this message: "No price too high." Elated, she purchased the bracelet. Needless to say, at her return her husband was dismayed. It was just a little thing--a comma--but what a difference it made!

This story says a lot about the importance of clear communication in marriage. Because we are different, there will be times when we experience breakdowns in marital communication. The more you communicate with your spouse, the more you will realize that somewhere in the middle, things can, and often will, get lost in delivery.

How do we mitigate the chances of our communication "packages" being lost in delivery? Well, I suggest that we view marital communication as a special delivery. From 1885 to 1997, the United States Postal Service offered special delivery whereby packages were dispatched more immediately and directly from the receiving post office to the recipient rather than being put in the mail for distribution on the regular delivery route. Special delivery required special handling, expedited delivery, and a higher cost than regular delivery. There are two components of special delivery that we should apply to all marital communication: Special handling and the willingness to pay the extra cost. When it comes to marital communication, the primary goal is not how fast the sender can get the message across to the recipient, but how the sender can assure that the message gets to the recipient safe and sound. It may cost more, but the investment will produce great dividends in your relationship.

When couples communicate, they should view the encounter as a special time of learning, appreciating, listening, encouraging, and connecting. When successful communication takes place, each of these components is achieved. Successful and effective marital communication is to marriage what blood is to life. Without it, a marriage will cease to function. Have you ever thought about it in that way? It is impossible to have a loving, thriving, biblical-modeling marriage without effective marital communication. Love cannot replace communication. Wealth cannot replace communication. Sex cannot replace communication. Without successful and effective communication, your marriage will cease to function the way God intended.

The number one key to any successful relationship is the ability to adequately communicate thoughts from one person to another. It is important that both parties recognize that it is never okay that only one person is doing all the communicating, because like the tango, it takes two. I must admit, communication is an area I (Walter) struggle with.

I am an introvert. I love spending time by myself. It's not that I don't enjoy being around people, but I prefer being alone in a calm, quiet, relaxing space. That's just me. Tarsha often says that if I had to live on the moon by myself, I'd be just fine, and she's right. However, she loves to talk, and prefers to talk to me. So, I have to constantly remind myself that communicating with me is a need of hers that I should strive to meet because I love her. While meeting that need is a work in progress for me, it is a special delivery cost that I'm willing to pay!

When I say "communicate with me," I don't mean her talking while I sit there, nod my head and smile. I mean communicating back and forth, contributing verbally and non-verbally to the conversation, no matter what the subject matter. Now does it get difficult sometimes? You bet. Has it been a source of my receiving the cold shoulder? More times than I can count. There have been times that we have driven 20-30 minutes without saying a word in the car, and when I realized it, all I could do was apologize, to which she would say in her sweet, gentle voice, "That's okay baby, I'm just glad you recognized it." It is here that I do my best to start talking. About what? Anything. I look for billboards, anything to converse about. This usually brings a smile to her face as well as spark some of our most hilarious conversations.

It doesn't take a lot to talk to your spouse because every conversation does not have to be a serious one. What makes communication in marriage so difficult is when each party becomes overly focused on talking about serious issues like bills, work, children, church, and the like. Effective communication is developed in the safety of talking about things that don't matter. Yes, you read that correctly! Sometimes you have to talk about things that really don't matter. Early on in our marriage, my father shared that helpful bit of advice with us and it has made such a difference. It's been through talking about things that really don't matter that we've learned to communicate verbally and nonverbally, attaining the outcomes of understanding and acceptance that are crucial for a healthy, lasting, and loving relationship. I have discovered that healthy communication allows the other person to state his/her intent regarding a matter instead of the other trying to read into what has been said. When we try to read intent, more often than not, we read it incorrectly.

This is one of the pitfalls of social media today. Partnerships and friendships have been ruined because someone misread the intent of an email, tweet, or post. Today, many forge relationships and even grow them through social media. As I speak with the generations that have come after me, many of them feel as though people no longer need a personal handshake or face-to-face meeting to effectively communicate. While I choose not to debate this issue here, I still believe that actually talking to a real person, using real words, in the presence of that person, is still the best way to get to know them, especially when it comes to the person you have vowed to spend the rest of your life with. Trying to read intent through a few typed words in the heat of an argument can be detrimental. Don't do it! Communicating in this manner may seem old-fashioned, but I believe it's still the best and most effective way to communicate and gain the correct intent of a person's heart, especially your spouse.

COMPONENTS OF COMMUNICATION

Throughout our many years of encouraging couples, it has been made perfectly clear that the greatest hurdle to overcome is ineffective communication. I can't count the number of cases where I have sat with a couple and listened to their marital challenges. Whether the discussion centered on financial mismanagement, lack of intimacy, lack of respect, or even sexual dysfunction, the root cause the majority of the time has been ineffective communication. If you want to enjoy a great marriage, let me tell you, effective communication is the key. You may be wondering why I keep referring to ineffective communication and effective communication, here's why.

As I was counseling a couple one day, I shared with them that what I assessed to be the issue was their consistent ineffective communication. Having observed them together in public and private, I discovered that yelling, criticizing, and blatant disrespectful non-verbals were their means of communication. Now, when I broached the subject of ineffective communication with them, they both suggested that they did not have a problem communicating with each other. "We talk all the time." It became crystal clear that they did not have a clue. In order for you to have a great marriage, simply talking is not enough. A lot of people talk all the time but have nothing to say and no one is listening. You must be able to effectively communicate with your spouse in a way that both of you feel loved, respected, and listened to.

Effective marital communication takes place when the three components of delivery are executed properly. It took a great deal of practice before I was able to successfully navigate the three components in our marital communication, and I must admit, I am still working on it. Albert Mehrabian in his book *Silent Messages* [8], assigns importance to the three components with percentages that indicate how much of the message is sent through each one. We have intentionally chosen not to list the percentages because of our respect for the research process that he engaged in and our understanding that the research conclusions were not strictly

---

[8] Mehrabian, A. (1981). Silent messages: Implicit communication of emotions and attitudes (2d ed.). Belmont, Calif.: Wadsworth Pub.

applicable to even the majority of conversations that most of us engage in. The main reason we are referencing the research however is to remind you of the components of communication and how important it is for you to understand that each component plays a role when you are seeking to improve in the area of effective communication with your spouse.

1. The first component is categorized as actual content. The actual content is the words that come out of our mouths. As previously stated, early on in our marriage, my father shared that great communication is learned through talking about those things that really don't matter. I believe his bit of advice speaks to a great marital principle: What you talk about is not as important as simply talking to one another.

Talk about anything and everything, so when big things come up, the foundation of trust and understanding will have already been laid, and communicating on the tough issues will be easier. Try it; it really works!

2. The second component is categorized as tone of voice. When we talk about tone of voice, we are talking about things such as volume and harshness. Some people brag about their ability to cut others with their words. Listen, if you truly love your spouse, why would you want to cut them in any way?

When it comes to tone, the last person to recognize there is a problem is the person with the tone problem. I can't count the number of times I've heard a spouse say to the other that "there is nothing wrong with my tone. You are just overly sensitive or I don't yell at you! That's just the way I talk." Let's be honest, in the heat of conflict, rarely do any of us pay attention to tone because we are more focused on our "comebacks." So, in order to ensure you are effectively communicating in the area of tone, I recommend that couples record a few of their conversations, play them back, and evaluate their individual tone of voice alone, and then with their spouse. The response we get from the overwhelming majority after practicing this step is, "I didn't know." Here is a rule of thumb that will help you here: if your spouse says you yell , 9.9 times out of 10, THEY ARE RIGHT!

3. **The third component is categorized as nonverbal communication.** Facial expressions, body posture, and actions fall into this category. Has your spouse ever said this to you, "Look at me when I'm talking to you"? That one stings, doesn't it? That statement has caused a great deal of chaos all over this world. Brothers, take my advice, if you are tired of hearing these words, you should avoid looking out the window while your wife is talking to you. That's some free advice. Take it, it will bless your life!

Before I share what God's word says about communication, allow me to make a crucial observation. We have noticed in many marriages that the individuals have been unaware that their negative interactions were much higher than their positive interactions. If this is true in your marriage, your relationship will suffer because the relationship will be viewed as negative by one or both of you. When the relationship is viewed as negative, negative interactions become the expected norm and hope for the future of the relationship dwindles, and is even lost. But there is good news! The word of God gives us a host of instructions on how to keep our interactions positive, loving, peaceful, and godly.

God's Word on Communication

When it comes to great communicators, I believe that there is none greater than the One true God who dwells in heaven. In fact, everything we see and even what we don't see is the result of His communication. God said, "Let there be", and it was. Talk about effective communication! What would happen in your marriage if you could so effectively communicate your thoughts and feelings, your expectations and directions to your spouse in such a way that every time you communicated with him/her, the result was, "and it was." Well, if you are still living on planet earth, you know that this outcome will not always be the case. However, the Great Communicator teaches us in His word some key principles that make for effective and successful communication not just in our marriages, but in life in general.

> *Rash language cuts and maims, but there is healing in the words of the wise.* (Proverbs 12:18 MSG)

> *Kind words heal and help; cutting words wound and maim.* (Proverbs 15:4 MSG)

> *The heart of the godly thinks carefully before speaking; the mouth of the wicked overflows with evil words.* (Proverbs 15:28 NLT)

> *If you listen to constructive criticism, you will be at home among the wise.* (Proverbs 15:28, 31 NLT)

> *People with understanding control their anger; a hot temper shows great foolishness.* (Proverbs 14:29 NLT)

> *Everyone enjoys a fitting reply; it is wonderful to say the right thing at the right time!* (Proverbs 15:23 NLT)

> *Those who control their tongue will have a long life; opening your mouth can ruin everything.* (Proverbs 13:3 NLT)

A gentle answer deflects anger, but harsh words make tempers flare.
(Proverbs 15:1 NLT)

A fool is quick-tempered, but a wise person stays calm when insulted.
(Proverbs 12:16 NLT)

Great marriages don't happen by accident. They take hard work and persistence in doing those things that bring about the desired results. When marriages lose love and hope, couples stop working on the relationship believing if they simply avoid conflict, the marriage will self-correct. I'm sorry, it is not that easy. Couples can't simply hope themselves into a good or great marriage, they have to put the necessary work in to assure the broken places are mended, and healthy communication is a key in turning your marriage around.

Learning to effectively communicate with your spouse requires patience, understanding, and a commitment to dwell together with your spouse in love. Yes, it is hard work. Yes, it will come at a great cost. But think about the feeling you get when you receive a package marked "Special Delivery" from someone who loves you. You can provide that special feeling to your spouse when you commit to communicate in such a way that assures the package gets to its destination safe and sound.

Think About This:

How far back would you have to go to recall a situation that illustrated great communication with your spouse on a difficult topic? How far back for a situation where the communication was not so great?

Write About This:

1. When you communicate with your spouse, for what percentage of your conversations is your cell phone, computer, or other electronic device within your reach?

   _____

   _____

2. What percentage of the time do you find yourself listening to them and still doing something else (cooking, surfing the Internet, watching TV, caring for a child, doing laundry, etc.)?

   _____

   _____

3. What percentage of the time do you think you are being fully attentive to the conversation?

   _____

   _____

4. What percentage of the time do you think your spouse would say you are fully engaged and attentive to the conversations you have?

   _____

   _____

5. What are you willing to do immediately to increase the amount of time that you are actively listening and participating in interactions with your spouse?

    _____

    _____

    _____

    _____

    _____

Have Fun With This:

Turn to a page in this book...yes, any page... and circle 5 **action** words on the page. (For example one of the pages I just turned to contains words like "charge," "judge," "wear," "take," and "hold").

COMMUNICATE each one of the words you circled without actually saying the word. Use your own rules such as acting out the word without speaking or trying to get the other person to guess the word without you actually saying the word but you are allowed to use synonyms or fill in the blank phrases that would allow them to guess it. Are you reading the book alone? Well get in front of a mirror and act out each word you choose. Go ahead! It's just for fun!

HER STUFF, HIS STUFF

HAVE YOU EVER SAT AND WATCHED TWO CHILDREN playing together? It can be hilarious. Children are quick to turn their focus from the toy they are playing with to one that another child is playing with. Often, this results in a tug-of-war where one ends up crying and yelling, "mine!" It's not unusual for a child to play with a toy, lose interest in it, lay it to the side, and begin to play with another toy. But as soon as that child sees another child heading for that toy, he/she races to retrieve the toy with a gesture that says, "You can't play with this one because it's mine."

We expect this type of behavior from children. It's a part of learning how to play well and share with others. But what happens in a marriage when one or both individuals decide that there are certain aspects of their lives that only belong to them?

When a husband and wife have separate bank accounts, separate friends, and separate places of worship, they run the risk of creating completely separate lives. When God ordained marriage, He said "and they shall become one flesh." God's idea of marriage is that of a man and woman sharing their new life together to the point that what's mine is hers and what's hers is mine. Some have resolved that marriage means what's mine is mine and what's theirs is mine. Let me assure you, that will not work in marriage.

When we got married, we brought things to the marriage. Credit card debt, student loans, and other debts. We soon realized that her student loan was no longer her student loan, it was our student loan. My Visa bill was not just my bill, it was ours. You see, if we are one, then there is no separation of assets or liabilities. It's all ours.

Coming to this point in any relationship can be challenging. Why? Well, because for so long, each of you has had his/her own things. You have been responsible for making decisions for yourself only. You have become comfortable with putting something in a place and knowing it will be there when you need it again. Any slight change in any of those dynamics can be quite unnerving. After 25 years of marriage, you would think I would have this down by now. Hey, don't judge me, I'm still working on it! I like to know where things are when I need them, and prefer them where I left them. Tarsha has a habit (it seems) to always unplug my phone to use whatever charger I was using to charge her phone. Never mind the fact that in the house there are at any given time 3-5 other working chargers that she can use. When asked about this, her only response is, "baby, your phone is almost fully charged anyway." What I want to say in those moments is "just use one of the other one million chargers we have in the house" (but I can't say that, and I don't recommend you say that either). It's in moments like these that I simply have to say, it's hers, she can use it anytime she wants. When she wears my Funky Socks with her boots, (and listen, I am very protective of my Funky Socks), I've learned to say to myself with joy, they are hers, she can wear them anytime. When she takes the vehicle with gas and leaves me with the one she left on empty, all I can say is, it's hers, she can drive whatever vehicle she wants to. I know it sounds crazy, but it is better this way and the benefits are out of this world ladies and gentlemen! This perspective eliminates arguments and hurt feelings as a result of one spouse feeling that there are certain things in their spouse's life that are off limits.

I once sat with a couple and the husband was enraged with his wife for opening a piece of "his mail." While she explained it was by accident, I was shocked to hear that since they were married, that was a standing rule of his that she was not to open any of "his" mail. Now I don't know how you feel about that, but this has trouble written all over it. Think of the suspicion this breeds. Is he hiding something? Who or what is he protecting? Is he in some type of trouble? Listen, it's not worth it. I want to encourage you to be open and share EVERYTHING with your spouse. Your email password, debit card PIN, all of it. Why? I'll tell you why. You wouldn't hide any of those things from yourself would you? No! To do so would allow us to classify you as insane. But when you hide things from your spouse or do not allow him/her access to certain things, that's literally what you are doing: Hiding things from yourself. So I say to you, if there are any areas in your life that have been deemed inaccessible to your spouse, unlock them today and grant your spouse unlimited access.

Remember this: Marriage is about combining, divorce is about dividing. The more you can share together, the stronger your marriage will be.

Think About This:

What is an area of your life that you feel only belongs to you? Is it an area that you feel should be shared with your spouse? Why or why not? Would God agree with the response you gave?

Write About This:

1. Sharing your passwords to your phone, email or banking websites may not be a challenge for you, but sharing your feelings may be a little more difficult. Not only does personal information like passwords and material things like cars, food, and homes belong to both spouses, but your heart belongs to your partner as well. Write about a time that it was difficult to share with your spouse your heart or your true feelings on a matter. Talk about this with them.

    _____

    _____

    _____

    _____

    _____

2. How did it feel as you anticipated having the conversation above?

    _____

    _____

    _____

Have Fun With This:

Fill in the blank.

My most treasured material possession is _____.

See if you can guess how your spouse would fill in their blank.

How did you do guessing what they treasure the most?

WHEN SEASONS CHANGE

Marriage is about figuring out how to make it through when things change. (Season 1 Episode 10 Lie To Me 19:17 secs)

MOST MODERN DAY CALENDARS DIVIDE THE YEAR INTO 4 seasons: winter, spring, summer, and fall (autumn). The dates that the seasons begin and end will vary depending on who you consult. However, one thing is for sure, seasons change. Because of the earth's axial tilt, it orbits the sun on a slant which means different areas of the earth point toward or away from the sun at different times of the year. Studies have shown that the changing of the seasons may have an impact on human health and well-being.

According to a study published in Nature Communications, the way your DNA functions (thanks to a process called gene expression) changes as the seasons do. In the winter, when the weather gets colder outside, increased inflammation often results. The change is designed to help your body be better equipped to fight off colds and flus. According to the Mayo Clinic, cold weather may cause your blood pressure to spike, in part due to the narrowing of blood vessels that happen in colder temperatures. In the summer, your cells are instructed to retain water and burn fat. That's right, your actual DNA changes when the weather changes. Both hypersomnia (which is the opposite of insomnia) and seasonal allergies often caused by pollinating plants can peak in the fall when the air starts to crisp up. Researchers have shown that participants in sleep studies slept nearly three hours more each day in October than any other time of the year. Suicide rates rise and fall as the weather changes, as well. A study published in Epidemiology found that in the northern hemisphere, when it's sunniest in the summer, suicide rates peak in June, while in the southern hemisphere, where seasons are flipped, suicide rates peak in December.

We experience the different natural seasons and the effects to our health and well-being simply because the earth spins around the sun at an angle. What an incredible metaphor for marriage! Like the earth is always spinning, so are our marriages. We get married, and the early excitement is off the charts. That's a season. Children are introduced into the equation. That's a season. The purchase of the first home, profession change, relocating of the family— these are all seasons. Health challenges- that's a season. Loss of job- that's a season. Major misunderstandings or bad decisions by one or both spouses- that is a season. Children move away and start their own families- yes, that's a season. The changing of seasons is a part of life, and just like seasons, everything in life changes. We know this, but still change often catches us by surprise and ill prepared. Why is that? Well, I believe it is the result of our living more as reactive beings than proactive beings in life in general, and especially in marriages.

In 1987, American girl group Expose's debut album featured a song written and produced by Lewis A. Martinee entitled "Seasons Change." Here is an excerpt:

> *Some dreams are in the night time, and some seem like yesterday*
> *But leaves turn brown and fade, ships sail away.*
> *You long to say a thousand words, but seasons change.*
> *It feels like it's forever, no reason for emptiness.*
> *But time just runs away, no more day by day.*
> *You dream again it seems in vain, when seasons change.*
> *Seasons change, feelings change, it's been so long since I found you.*
> *Yet it seems like yesterday.*
> *Seasons change, people change, I'll sacrifice tomorrow, just to have*
> *you here today.*[9]

The song poetically depicts the fading away of a relationship caused by changes brought by time and the changes that occur with people. Let's be clear, everything around us changes. The phone you have today will be obsolete in a matter of months, even weeks. Yet we look forward to the changes that the manufacturer calls upgrades. No one uses 8-tracks anymore. As a matter of fact, CDs have all but become obsolete with the evolution of Apple music, and multiple other streaming platforms. Do we complain about the changes? Well, some do, but the reality is that if we want to enjoy the times we live in, we must adjust to the changes or be helplessly left behind.

In our marriages, a host of changes will occur based on the simple fact that people change. As we get older, we become wiser. As we get older, what once mattered to us no longer seems that important. As we

---

[9] https://www.azlyrics.com/lyrics/expose/seasonschange.html

get older, some of the foolishness that we were willing to overlook and put up with earlier in the relationship, we will do so no longer. However, instead of viewing the changes as unwelcomed house guests, we should view them as marital upgrades, opportunities to take our marriages to the next level and experience other aspects of marriage that we've never experienced before. The sad truth is that when many begin to experience change in their marriage, they subconsciously equate it with unhappiness. The overwhelming outcome of equating change with unhappiness is the emotional response, "I don't feel like I'm married anymore." I can't tell you how many times I've heard this from couples who have been married twenty, thirty, and even forty years. When we are not committed to a positive, proactive response to change in our relationships, it is inevitable that the "I don't feel like" monster will raise its ugly head and you will find your marriage on a downward slope filled with sharp edges and deep ravines. If you've ever been hiking, you know that sharp edges and deep ravines are both painful and terrifying. So how do we navigate the changing seasons of marriage without losing passion for our spouse and hope for the future?

Well, the starting point is a piece of wisdom I heard years ago during a men's conference. The speaker that night was Bishop Joseph Garlington, Sr., the Senior Pastor of Covenant Church of Pittsburgh. During his message, Bishop Garlington shared about a time he expressed to his wife that he didn't feel like he was married. To his surprise, his wife replied, "Adjust your feelings to the facts!" That response is forever solidified in my consciousness. You see, no matter how we feel, the truth remains the same, we are married. I can be mad as hell at Tarsha, but that doesn't change the fact that we are married. I could have said the most inappropriate and crushing thing to her and she to me, but it does not change the fact that we are married.

A key to managing changing seasons in marriage is to never allow feelings to override sound judgement. Many have made life altering decisions based on feelings, only to look back and admit that the decision they made was the wrong one. A bit of advice here is that whenever you find yourself in a place where you are contemplating a decision based on feelings, adjust your feelings to the fact that you are married and what you have committed to: "Until death do us part." Looking back over our 25 years of marriage, I can clearly identify the seasons of our marriage. Unlike the consistency of the meteorological seasons, marital seasons will vary in length, scope, and intensity, and the reality is whether it is a good season for you or a difficult one, it will not last always.

The Difficult Seasons

The first three years of our marriage were hard to say the least. When I consider what a miracle is, I classify the fact that we are still together a miracle. We started off with our two-year old son, meager incomes as teachers, the arrival of our second son ten months later, and the reality of truly getting to know the "real" person that we had married. Let me tell you, at times, we both felt like we had made a terrible mistake. I was selfish; she was very, very, very opinionated. I was soft spoken; she was a professional in using vocabulary words not found in the 23rd Psalm. I was a spendthrift; she was a penny pincher. I was carefree, she was a worrywart. Each of these differences made for the perfect storm. We argued about everything and blamed each other for the difficulties we were experiencing. I tell you, it was tough. So tough, that one Sunday morning, as we were on our way to church, I turned to Tarsha and said, " I want a divorce." I was tired of being unhappy. I was tired of the fighting. I was tired of being broke. I was tired of trying to make the marriage work. It seemed hopeless. The difficult seasons are ones that cause pain and frustration. You will likely not want to devote any effort to bettering what may seem like a hopeless situation. When those are your feelings, you are likely in one of perhaps several difficult seasons that you will experience in your marriage, but these are the times to talk out your feelings with a seasoned individual who can guide you and pray with you. There will be seasons in your relationship when better seems unattainable. In those season, strive to put your spouse's needs ahead of your wants and preferences; believe that better is possible.

The Learning Seasons

If you started a garden, then looked at it after six months or a year, and it was brown, how would you assess the condition? Well, if you don't take care of your marriage, the same thing will happen. So, if you moved to another location, started another garden with the same process you employed with the previous garden, should you expect a different result?

This is what the learning seasons in our marriage teach us. I say teach instead of taught because the learning seasons never end. We learned and resolved that divorce is not an option. I truly believe that a key to a great marriage is an early commitment from both husband and wife that divorce is not an option. In fact, we resolved to never mention the word divorce again to the point that when we reference divorce in any conversation we are having, we say "the D word" (we will discuss in another chapter). I believe that too many people believe if they can plant a garden somewhere else, things will be better, not accepting that the problem is with the soil.

In Mark 4:3-9, Jesus tells the parable of the sower. In Mark 4:13-20, He explains it. The parable describes four types of soil. Take a moment to read those passages now before continuing with your reading here.

1. The wayside soil represents a heart that has no real interest in God. This type of heart produces skepticism and a lack of understanding. People with this type of heart have a hard time receiving truth. It is difficult to get a person with this type of heart to let go of their old faulty belief systems and embrace new ones. This is often seen in the marital relationship when a spouse cannot accept feedback. It is also demonstrated by those who say things like "this is just the way I am or I was never taught how to..."

2. The rocky soil represents people whose hearts have been hardened by major sin issues and emotional wounds. The hardened heart usually produces an unstable and weak mind. They rarely love to the extent that they are compelled to persevere through challenges. They are quick to suggest separation or divorce and will often point to ways they have been the victim in past and present relationships.

3. The thorny soil represents a heart that receives truth readily and with joy, but because it is so attached to things, as time goes on, the cares, the riches of the world, and the busyness of life cause them to lose interest in the things of God. When we as married couples start out, we most often do so with the intent of doing everything possible to create and maintain a vibrant relationship. At times, good things like taking care of children, working longer hours, or even serving community or church groups take priority over what God has said should be number one after Him and that is your spouse. If this is you, your heart is represented by thorny soil.

4. The good soil represents a heart that is receptive to God's perspective on matters. Not only does this type of heart welcome His perspective, but the perspective is lived out. As a result, fruit is produced in the person's life. This type of heart is present in one who - when they learn better, they do better. They recognize that they are not perfect and that they can always do more to strengthen their relationship with their spouse.

As the parable describes what happens when different types of hearts encounter the Word of God, the learning seasons help us identify where we are and where our hearts are regarding our spouses and the institution of marriage. When our hearts are out of alignment with God's view of marriage, no amount of effort from the other will be able to have a positive impact on the relationship. When it comes to a garden, the problem is never with the seed, it is always with the soil. In a marriage, the problem is never with God's design for marriage, it is always with whether we engage in it our way or God's way. Our way results in little or no fruit. God's way results in much fruit.

The state of our hearts will determine the type of marriage we will have. The reality is that we determine what type of soil our heart will be. We determine whether we will have a wayside, rocky, thorny, or good heart. What God says about marriage will not produce fruit in our lives until it is planted in a heart that is receptive and obedient. If you are going to have a great marriage, you have to consistently cultivate the condition of your heart as well as contribute to the healthy cultivation of your spouse's heart. Remember, the problem is never with the seed. When there is a problem, it is with the soil.

What do your actions, behavior, and reactions to various marital and non-marital situations reflect about your heart attitude? When you are intentional and consistent about answering this question to learn more about how to successfully navigate the marriage journey, you are in the learning season. Most successful couples will find themselves in the learning seasons multiple times throughout the marriage.

The Applying and Fruitful Seasons

Here is where marriage gets good! You have learned what makes your spouse tick. You have learned what rubs them the wrong way. You have learned what turns them on romantically, now, it's time to put it into action.

During the learning seasons, I am constantly learning what Tarsha perceives as me yelling at her and how that makes her feel. So, the applying seasons are the times that if she says I am yelling, my only response is "I'm sorry." In the applying season, I made sure I took as much weight off of her by washing clothes, feeding the kids before she got home from work, and as often as I could, ensured she had dinner ready for her after a long day. It's been said, when you learn better, you should do better. That's what the applying and fruitful seasons are all about. Put what you have learned through the ups and downs into practice. You know how it felt to have to go through the learning process, now it's time to enjoy the fruit of enduring the difficult and learning seasons. Enjoy the fruit of her smile after you have cleaned up the house. Enjoy your spouse's ability to enjoy a peaceful afternoon or weekend void of any household responsibilities.

The applying and fruitful seasons are worth having to learn the lessons of cultivating a strong marriage, because from your spouse's perspective, when they know you have learned and are putting the lessons into practice, they will withhold no good thing from you!

Now, I must share this bit of truth with you as well. Marriage is often cyclical. You will not always live in the applying and fruitful seasons. Sometimes it will feel as though both of you have forgotten what it means to be married, but this is not the time to get down on yourselves, it is, however, the time for you to recognize you may be experiencing a difficult season. Take confidence in this, you made it before, and you'll make it again.

As you journey on this road of marriage, trust and believe that the good will outweigh the bad. And while difficult seasons will arise in your marriage, just like every storm, they will pass, and you will be made the better for having gone through and come out together.

Think About This:

Based upon temperature readings and the weather conditions normally occurring in various seasons, would you classify your marriage right now as one that is in winter, summer, spring or fall?

Write About This:

1. What advice would you give to someone who is in the "difficult season" of marriage?

    _____

    _____

    _____

    _____

    _____

2. Write a prayer thanking God, asking forgiveness from God, or seeking guidance from God in regards to the type of heart you have as it relates to your marriage.

_____

_____

_____

_____

_____

_____

_____

_____

Challenge: share the prayer with your spouse and ask that they join you over the next week in going before God in the various areas you brought up.

Have Fun With This:

Pretend you are in your fifth grade science class. Grab a cup, some soil and a bean (lima or pinto beans work well). Plant it, care for it and see whether you or your spouse can care better for the seed which will sprout fairly soon!

BEST FRIENDS

THERE IS A PERSON THAT I ABSOLUTELY LOVE HANGING out with. When we are together we don't necessarily have to talk a lot but when we do talk, it is oftentimes about the most random things. There is a person who has gone on trips with me to places that neither of us had been and we were like two lost sheep just wandering around together but not stressing because we knew ultimately that if something horribly wrong took place, at least we would be experiencing it together. The friend that I am talking about also laughed at me when I couldn't catch on as quickly as others to new skills that we were being taught like salsa dancing, shooting guns or painting.

The funny thing is that any sentence in the last paragraph could have been written by either of us because they are the opinions of two people who are best friends. When a husband or wife intentionally sets out to establish a friendship with their spouse, she finds herself sharing a little bit less on a regular basis with her girlfriends and he spends less time disclosing those more personal details with his buddies. Before you decide to skip this chapter, let me mention now that I am not saying that you should not have friends outside of your spouse. Many of us have friendships that were formed in childhood and they are healthy and vibrant friendships. These relationships are with people who have proven that they would be with you through tough times and great times, through times that you rejoiced and times that you cried, through promotions and terminations as well as through births and deaths. I am not suggesting that these friendships end, I am suggesting that the same level of effort and approaches made to establish the foundations of those friendships be pursued in the confines of the marital relationship.

Think about this—you are close to your best friend because of things like: the secrets that you have shared, the amount of time that you have spent with one another and the things that you have tried together. Also consider that if you have strong feelings about things that your spouse has done or said and you are sharing those things **exclusively** with a friend **outside** of your marriage, which relationship results in stronger levels of communication? The more you communicate with someone, especially in regards to exchanging information about feelings, beliefs and opinions (versus superficial communication like food, weather and daily events), the more likely you are to build firm foundations for friendship and true relationship. When the friend, coworker, or relative outside the marriage is the primary person with whom you share the deeper details, many times that release of information, venting and sharing is sufficient for you; however, the opportunity for "friendship building" with **the spouse** is not made available from that situation. In other words, your improved skills in expressing your thoughts and emotions are all benefiting your relationship with the person with whom you shared those thoughts and feelings. Why not allow your friendship with your spouse to be established and strengthened in the same manner? You want to become closer friends with your spouse? Then make a plan to intentionally choose them as the first person with whom you share your thoughts about things that make you happy and things that make you hurt, things that inspire you and things that scare you, things that make you angry as well as things that brighten your day.

Not only does deep and meaningful communication assist in laying the groundwork for friendship, but the amount of time spent with someone is also a contributing factor. Many marital relationships today consist of two people who are only like two ships passing in the night. They see each other but only briefly and only vaguely. This is especially true for those couples that are immersed in a dual income family and have small children who are involved in a variety of activities.

Being raised in a household where he was the oldest of 3 very athletic boys, my husband was undoubtedly ecstatic when we had our first son and then when we rounded it out a little over 3 and a half years later with yet another son. (I certainly would not attempt to get a girl with a third pregnancy; I saw how that worked out for his mother!) While I was one of five children, who had a variety of skill levels in various sports, my siblings and I also enjoyed participating in the arts and music. I ran track in high school and I liked to go to football and basketball games. It seemed that soon after each of our sons started walking, each began getting involved in sports. Between the time Walter spent coaching them and the time they all spent in front of the television either watching sports or playing sports-based video games, the sole female in the house seemed to be someone who was not intentionally ignored, but was getting about as much attention as the floral sofa that no one could sit on in the front room. If I wanted to make sure I stopped being ignored, I had to pull out the big guns. I needed to make a decision that I would not complain, but instead learn the game! And so my mission began. I would not bid them farewell when it was time for soccer practice or tee ball practice. If he wanted to coach every single season for every single sport (yes, even those he had never played), I would be right there as the team mom, the team manager, the water girl or whatever was needed to get me right there on the sidelines with him. Between games, whether at dinner or on rides to practices, we would discuss strategy and laugh about the never-ending material provided by 4 and 5 year old emerging sports stars. On Sunday afternoons during football season, I decided not to be the typical wife who complained about not having a husband for 4 months a year, but instead I put my basic knowledge of the game to use and strategically interjected phrases like, "I'm not sure I'd pass the ball on 2nd and 3." Talk about a turn on for him! Who needs to watch the game with a basement full of guys when your wife has a skill set like that!

For about 18 years beginning when our oldest son was old enough to hold a basketball and think he could dribble with it and ending when our youngest son ran his last lap around the track, we were parents that did our best to get our children to practices, meets and games, volunteer to assist coaches, provide team snacks and whatever else was needed to contribute to their individual and the team's success. What started as an attempt for me to be more involved in the extracurricular activities of my sons and an attempt for me to see how I could increase the time that my husband and I were together, has consequently allowed for us to now have sports as an area that we spend hours each week talking about. It has resulted in our going to sporting events multiple times a year and making memories together. Additionally, we use our enjoyment of sports and physical activity to come together for exercising and thus we help each other become more physically fit.

Indeed as I think about the benefits I thought I would reap when I first packed up a chair to sit on the sideline at the first game he coached, I am amazed at all the *added* benefits experienced by my making myself available and showing interest in an area that we have now bonded over in so many ways. What can be that area for you? Try to identify an area that your spouse is extremely interested in and maybe you are not. How can you make attempts at showing interest or learning more about it? You might be surprised how you now have another topic that you can use to develop your communication with each other and increase your quality time together. Time, communication, and shared interests are so important to building strong friendships. A strong friendship between spouses is absolutely essential to the making of a strong marriage.

Whether you have children or not, every couple should strive to spend as much time together as possible doing things that create lasting memories. During our early years and during the formative years of our sons, Walter had three jobs. While countless hours were dedicated to lesson plans, investigative reports, and strategic planning for children and youth programs, he often remarks that what he remembers most about those days were the trips taken with just the two of us, the family weekend get-a-ways to San Antonio, the cruises, and the trips to competitions for our sons' various track and basketball teams. It was during those memorable experiences that our friendship deepened. We laughed a lot. We problem-solved together. We simply recognized more and more how blessed we were to have each other not just as a spouse, but also as a friend. As we continue on this journey, every future experience will be another opportunity to learn something new about this best friend that God has given each of us. Challenge yourself to allow your moments spent together to become the fruitful place whereby your friendship is taken to unimaginable heights and depths.

Think About This:

Who do you talk to most about your beliefs and feelings regarding the deeper issues in life? Who do you talk to most about struggles you experience?

Write About This:

1. What qualities are present in long-lasting, healthy friendships? Name as many as you can.

_____

_____

_____

_____

_____

_____

_____

_____

_____

_____

2. As you read each passage listed, write down something that comes
   to mind regarding friendship. Read Proverbs 18:24, Proverbs 17:9,
   Proverbs 17:17, Ecclesiastes 4:9 and 10

_____

_____

_____

_____

_____

_____

_____

3. Reflecting on your answers to questions 1 and 2, what are some
   areas that can be worked on as you and your spouse develop your
   friendship?

_____

_____

_____

_____

_____

_____

Have Fun With This:

A FRIENDLY COMPETITION! How many TV shows or movies can you name that were based on friendship between two or more people? Who was able to come up with the most in five minutes? If you get stuck for more than five minutes, do a quick search on the Internet.

THE D WORD

HERE ARE A FEW SAYINGS I'VE HEARD IN CONVERSATIONS about divorce over the years:

1. Divorce: When being told you're wrong every single day of your life just isn't working for you anymore.

2. Divorce: Better to have loved and lost, than live with a psycho for the rest of your life.

3. I am a marvelous housekeeper. Every time I leave a man I keep his house.

4. The only thing that keeps me from being happily married is my spouse.

5. Never lose yourself while trying to hold on to someone who doesn't even care about losing you.

6. At some point in every marriage there appears to be grounds for divorce. The trick is to continue to find grounds to stay together.

I shared in an earlier chapter that when we talk about divorce, we call it "the D word." After our marriage had gotten on the right track, we vowed that we would never again use that term as a weapon against one another. Even in casual conversation, if we have to use the term, we often say "the D word." For us, this designation reminds us that "the D word" will never be an option for us. Come hell or high water, we are stuck with each other, and we are okay with that!

We truly believe many couples consider "the D word" as an option when things get difficult because they don't understand what it is and why it was instituted. A proper understanding of "the D word" forces us to take a look at the condition of our heart and not what we think our spouse can do better to cause us to stick around. Let's briefly examine the history of "the D word" starting with the words of Jesus.

> *It was said, WHOEVER SENDS HIS WIFE AWAY, LET HIM GIVE HER A CERTIFICATE OF DIVORCE (Matthew 5:31).*

This text is found in the context of Jesus' teaching in the Sermon on the Mount. The Jewish audience recognized this declaration of Moses in Deuteronomy 24:1.

> *When a man takes a wife and marries her, and it happens that she finds no favor in his eyes because he has found some indecency in her,*

and he writes her a certificate of divorce and puts it in her hand and sends her out from his house...

The context of the Sermon on the Mount is the heart condition of kingdom citizens. Jesus makes it clear that it is not His intent to nullify Moses or any facet of the Law, but to fulfill or expose the true intention of the Law. Too often when people read "fulfill", they assume that Jesus was saying that He came to do the works of the law. That is incorrect. Jesus was saying that He came to reveal what the law meant and why it was given in the first place. In other words, Jesus came to give the spirit of the law by not stopping at what was said, but unpacking what was meant. Listen as Jesus unpacks the spirit of why Moses instituted "the D word":

> *He said to them, "Because of your hardness of heart Moses permitted you to divorce your wives; but from the beginning it has not been this way" (Matthew 19:8).*

In Moses's day, men were leaving their wives left and right for any reason they chose. A man could say three times, "I divorce you" and leave his wife to marry someone else. This left the woman in a dire situation because she could not remarry without a **bill of divorcement,** and many times, she did not have any means of support when her husband left.

That is the reason for the custom of taking the dowry (money given to her at marriage by her father) and exchanging that for coins to be worn around the neck or hung from headdresses. Then she would have finances if her husband put her out.

Or what woman, if she has ten silver coins and loses one coin, does not light a lamp and sweep the house and search carefully until she finds it? When she has found it, she calls together her friends and neighbors, saying, Rejoice with me, for I have found the coin which I had lost! (Luke 15:8-10)

Moses' intent was to ensure that wives who found themselves discarded by their husbands would not be left destitute. So, if men were going to leave their wives for any reason, they must give them a bill of divorcement, which was his way of protecting wives from husbands with cold and hard hearts.

When Jesus quotes Moses, he is making this point: What you think in your heart is as important as what you do. Jesus was saying that divorce is not the problem. The problem is what leads up to it. Divorce is the consequence of wrong attitudes and unhealthy expectations toward your spouse and the marriage covenant. Jesus points out that what Moses allowed because of hard hearts, God had never intended. God said not to let anyone separate the couple bonded together by covenant vows (Gen.2:21-25), and Jesus wanted us to contemplate what makes a marriage, not the reasons we can get out of a marriage.

Since October 2, 2003, a framed covenant agreement has hung on the wall in our bedroom. The agreement entitled Our Marriage Covenant, reads:

Believing that God, in His wisdom and providence, has established marriage as a covenant relationship, a sacred and lifelong promise, reflecting our unconditional love for one another and believing that God intends for the marriage covenant to reflect His promise to never leave us nor forsake us, We, the undersigned, do hereby reaffirm our solemn pledge to fulfill our marriage vows. Furthermore, we pledge to exalt the sacred nature and permanence of the marriage covenant by calling others to honor and fulfill their marriage vows.

When Tarsha and I signed this agreement in 2003 after eight years of marriage, we thought it fitting to do so in the presence of our two sons and have them sign it as well. We had them read it, we talked about it, and then they signed it as witnesses to their parents renewing their marital covenant. We wanted to assure our sons that their parents were serious about staying together. We wanted to model before our sons that when a man and woman pledge themselves together in marriage, that it is a promise that is not to be taken lightly. We wanted to assure our sons that no matter what their friends' parents were doing, they did not have to worry about their parents getting a divorce. I believe this is so important because when it comes to divorce, the children don't have a say, and often feel a sense of responsibility for the demolishment of their family. Not only must we commit to say no to divorce, but we should invite our children in as protectors of our marriage by giving them the assurance that they are allowed to ask questions and hold us accountable to our marriage vows.

A New Goal

If you are reading this book in the midst of contemplating divorce, I want you to know that you can turn your marriage around. However, you must also accept the fact that nothing turns around by itself. It will take work. It will take forgiveness. It will take patience. It will take open and loving communication. But even before all of that takes place, a first step will be required, and that first step is the setting of a new goal: The goal of reconciliation. If reconciliation is not at the heart of turning your marriage around, ultimately your attempt will fail. Setting the new goal of **reconciliation** is the commitment to replace the goal of **vindication** against your spouse for what they have done in the **past** with the goal to do whatever it takes to develop a stronger, less troubled marriage for **years to come**. Attaining this new goal will be challenging at times, but it is achievable when both parties are working towards the same goal. Allow me to offer some scriptural counsel on how you can achieve this goal of reconciliation in your marriage.

In his summary of the excellency of love, Paul offers these words in 1 Corinthians 13:13, " But now faith, hope, love, abide these three; but the greatest of these is love" (1 Corinthians 13:13, NASB). While this passage is known by many, it must be understood in the context of what has previously been addressed, and what has previously been addressed is the explanation of what love is. Paul uses fifteen descriptors to drive home the point that love is not a feeling, but action that flows out of a right heart attitude. Notice how Paul defines what love is in verses 4-7 from the New Living Translation:

1. Love is patient. Action!
2. Love is kind. Action!
3. Love is not jealous. Action!
4. Love is not boastful. Actions!
5. Love is not proud. Action!
6. Love is not rude. Action!
7. Love does not demand its own way. Action!
8. Love is not irritable. Action!
9. Love keeps no record of being wronged. Action!
10. Love does not rejoice about injustice. Action!

11. Love rejoices whenever the truth wins. Action!
12. Love never gives up. Action!
13. Love never loses faith. Action!
14. Love is always hopeful. Action!
15. Love endures through every circumstance. Action!

I believe Paul categorizes love as "the greatest of these" because without it and the actions that define it, faith is lifeless and hope is simply a dream. Use Paul's list to empower you in your fight against "The D Word." When you find yourself being impatient with the one you love, remind yourself that love is patient. When you find yourself bringing up the past in a present issue, remind yourself that love keeps no record of being wronged. When you ask yourself, what's the use, remind yourself that love never gives up, never loses faith, is always hopeful, and endures through every circumstance. You have what it takes to reach that new goal of reconciliation. Now go for it!

The Trilogy

So, what empowers us to achieve the goal of reconciliation? The trilogy of faith, hope, and love, working together with wisdom and understanding, is what makes it possible. When a marriage is on shaky ground, both parties must develop a confident expectation that things will get better. They must encourage one another to keep believing, no matter what! That's the <u>faith</u> dynamic. The faith dynamic is crucial because when people do not feel loved or valued, they tend to feel sad, jealous, resentful, angry, or bitter, which requires a decision to either respond in the flesh or respond in faith. When the choice is made time and time again to respond in the flesh, it becomes the prime opportunity to place "the D word" on the table. Allow this revelation to set you free— Responding in the flesh only leads to uglier emotions, but responding in faith empowers us to work through love to denounce the ugly emotions and promote an increased sense of value in our partner.

Secondly, both parties must be convinced that God will be with them through the difficult circumstances, even when He has not revealed a clear way around the circumstances. That's what having <u>hope</u> for a better marriage is all about. Like the three Hebrew boys, He walks through the furnace with us. Like the Israelites in captivity, He works hand in hand with us. Like Stephen standing in front of his enemies with stones in hand, He stands for us. That's the dynamic of hope that provides inspiration and motivation to persevere when we would otherwise throw in the towel. It's time to get your hope back. You may have been demotivated, demoralized and depressed, but the Holy Spirit is inspiring hope in you that is setting you on an upward trajectory of progress towards a great marriage. Believe it! Receive it.

Finally, both parties must commit to value and to avoid devaluing the other. This is done by adhering to the actions of <u>love</u> described by Paul in 1 Corinthians 13. This means that each partner must demonstrate how much the other is valued even when they don't feel like it. This means that neither partner will devalue the other when they feel the urge to lash out when they may have been wronged or even ignored. This is what Paul meant in Colossians 3:14 when he said, "Put on love, which is the perfect bond of unity." Remember, earlier in Colossians 3, Paul had written about the bad actions we should put off (fornication, uncleanness, passion, evil desire, covetousness, anger, wrath, malice, blasphemy, filthy language). Then he wrote about the good behavior we should put on (mercy, kindness, humility, meekness, longsuffering, bearing with one another, and forgiveness). Just when it appeared that Paul had emphatically made his point, he wrote this powerful sentence: "But above all these things put on love, which is the perfect bond of unity." Paul wanted us to know that even after we have taken off the bad and put on the good, the question still remains: *Have you put on love?*

No matter what else there is in your marriage, if you refuse to put on love, your relationship will be void of the greatest thing because love fulfills what God requires of the man and the woman in the covenant marital relationship. Love is the chain that ties a couple to God and each other. When Paul declares that love is the perfect bond of unity, he means that love brings people together and makes their differences compatible. In case you didn't know it, you are not your spouse and your spouse is not you. You are different, and different isn't a bad thing. Like a band or orchestra that consists of different instruments, when it plays together, the result is a pleasant sound. Love is the sound that each partner must play in order to produce the sound of marriage that God is listening for.

If divorce has been an option for you, pray for wisdom and strength to take it off the table in your marriage. Don't give the devil an opportunity to use that against you when tough times arise. Agree together that divorce/"the D word" will never again be an option in your marriage. Call upon the trilogy of faith, hope and love and watch how quickly things can turn around when you place then into any challenging situation you encounter.

Think About This:

What are your thoughts regarding divorce? Have your thoughts changed at any point in your life? Do you believe the marriages of people close to you during your childhood played any part in your thoughts regarding divorce?

Write About This:

1. Consider the statement "divorce is the consequence of wrong attitudes and unhealthy expectations towards your spouse in the marriage covenant." What could be an "unhealthy expectation" that one could have of their spouse?

    _____

    _____

    _____

2. Prayerfully consider your relationship with your mate. Do you think you have any unhealthy expectations of them?

    _____

    _____

    _____

3. What, if any, unhealthy expectations do they have of you?

    _____

    _____

    _____

4. Describe practical ways these unhealthy expectations can be dealt with so that the ultimate consequence is not divorce.

_____

_____

_____

_____

_____

_____

_____

Have Fun With This:

Act out (without using any words or sounds) one of the fifteen descriptors of "love." Allow 30 seconds for each person. Your partner has to guess which aspect of love you are trying to describe. Continue the activity until all 15 have been completed.

#Strong Marriages

A SOCIAL MEDIA HASHTAG IS A WORD OR PHRASE PRE-
ceded by what was once referred to as the pound symbol (#). Hashtags
categorize content. Click on a hashtag and you'll be able to browse
posts that have been tagged with it. Attach one to your own photo or
video and it will be discoverable to anyone searching the hashtag. How
likely it is to be seen by other users depends on how often the hashtag
is used, how popular your post is, and how strong your following is.
Ecclesiastes 4:9-12 says,

> *Two are better than one because they have a good return for their*
> *labor. For if either of them falls, the one will lift up his companion.*
> *But woe to the one who falls when there is not another to lift him*
> *up. Furthermore, if two lie down together they keep warm, but how*
> *can one be warm alone? And if one can overpower him who is alone,*
> *two can resist him. A cord of three strands is not quickly torn apart.*

Having discussed the issues of politics (4:1-3) and wealth (4:4-8), the writer shares his insights on friendship, and I believe those insights offer lifestyle marriage content that will make you a walking hashtag of what a strong marriage looks like. We discussed in the last chapter some of the ways to cultivate an environment where friendship grows. This chapter will highlight some traits present in a marriage between spouses who are truly friends of one another.

Solomon, one of the wisest persons to have lived, details several benefits of friendship:

1. Two can work better than one and so have a larger profit.
2. Friends can help each other in time of need.
3. Friends give emotional comfort to each other. The warmth of lying beside each other does not refer to sexual activity, nor are the two necessarily husband and wife. It is an image derived from that of travelers who must lie beside each other to stay warm on cold desert nights. But the usage here is metaphorical for emotional comfort against the coldness of the world.
4. Friends give each other protection; for that, in fact, a third friend is even better!

Strong marriages usually involve couples that are each other's best friend. There is a deeper level of trust and devotion associated with your best friend, and no one should enjoy more of your trust and devotion than your spouse. I am often asked who is my best friend, and without hesitation I say my wife. It is not unusual that my response is met with doubt and I understand why. I have not always been able to say that my wife is my best friend. Early on in our marriage, we were just trying to do enough to stay together. Of course we were living together, paying bills together, having children together, vacationing together, cuddling together, but none of these things had the power to make us friends. Proverbs 17:17 says, "A friend loves at all times; and a friend is born for adversity." I can say that this scripture caused me to shift my focus from Tarsha just being my wife to being my friend, and from my being my friend to being my best friend.

After the first three years of what we call the years from hell in our marriage, we began to recognize that we had come through so much together. All of the arguments, disappointments, and times contemplating divorce had become the seedbed that solidified to us that we were in this "till death do us part." Every time I thought about how much of my foolishness she had put up with, I knew I had to be more to her than just a typical husband. I decided from that point on that next to God, I would be her number one source of love and support. We began to talk more. We began to be more open and honest with each other. We became more vulnerable with each other to the point that we shared things that we had never shared with anyone else. The more of the "not so good" stuff we shared, the deeper our friendship grew. That's what real friendship is all about. When you have someone in your life that knows all about you but loves you unconditionally, that's friendship. We began lovingly telling each other the truth regardless of possible consequences. We began to unconditionally support the aspirations of the other, even if that meant me doing the laundry, helping the kids with their homework, and cooking dinner before she got home after a long day at the office. What I once looked at as things that I needed to do out of obligation, I began seeing as things that I did not only for my wife, but for my best friend.

When couples are each other's best friend, at least four things are present that make for a strong marriage.

1. *Strong marriages involve couples who are content to be alone with each other.*

For the past ten years or so, we have taken at least two trips each year with the intent to be with each other. At one point our friends thought we were moving to the Dominican Republic because we were spending so much time there. We looked forward to going there each year, and sometimes, twice in a year, just to enjoy some quality time alone with each other. Sitting on the beach talking for hours in that relaxed environment is priceless. Because we are not under any pressure to return calls or emails, our minds become solely tuned in to sharing and listening to one another. I can't recall a single time that either of us have said, "I can't wait to get back home." On the contrary, we always wish we could have stayed longer, simply enjoying one another.

I recognize that this is not the case with all couples. It has become the custom that when they go out for a night on the town or even an extended vacation, they invite others to join. Don't get me wrong, that is okay when the goal is to get away with friends and family, but you should make it a priority to get away with only your spouse as much as you can because it provides the space to get to know one another all over again.

Even if you can't be alone on a Caribbean vacation, you can be alone in the confines of your home just as well. Make a conscientious decision to give the best of yourself to your spouse recognizing that you can't do so when you are always around other people. Try setting aside weekends where you refrain from checking texts, emails, and other messages and devote that time to spend with your spouse and just talk. Share your hopes and dreams with one another. Play some games. Read a play, each pretending to be one of the characters. Take a walk together. Exercise together. Whatever you do, just make sure you are doing it together, alone with one another.

Those moments hold the potential for being some of the happiest and most rewarding times in your marriage. In our marriage, the times that we spend alone with each other draw us closer because our focus is solely on each other. The alone time serves as a space where I can listen to what has been on Tarsha's mind, and if there are things that I need to correct, I can take the necessary steps. Couples who have not spent the necessary time beyond the sexual attraction to develop a genuine friendship will find those alone times together hard to endure.

2. *Strong marriages involve couples that value one another for who they are on the inside, and not just how they look on the outside.*

Physical attraction (body shape, facial appearance, hair type, eye color) is one of the primary forces that draws two people together. For those of you who were around in the late 60s, these sultry words of one particular Motown song will mean something to you:

> *So in love, sad as could be, 'Cause a pretty face got the best of me. Suddenly, you came into my life, And gave it meaning and pure delight. Now, good looks, I've learned to do without, 'Cause now I know it's love that really counts. 'Cause I know that (Beauty's only skin deep, yeah, yeah, yeah) I know that (Beauty's only skin deep, oh yeah) yes indeed.*

My wife is gorgeous. It is what attracted me to her back in 1991. Her lips, her smile, her chocolate skin, my, my, my! I thank God that she is so attractive, but her inner beauty is attractive on another level.

When I say Tarsha is beautiful on the inside, I mean that she possesses a host of virtues that make her a loving and trustworthy person. When I see beyond her exterior beauty, I see the virtues of kindness, generosity, thoughtfulness, authenticity, and a desire to help others become all they can be, just to name a few.

I'll never forget Mother's Day 2020. We were in the midst of the Coronavirus pandemic and it was Whitney's, (my daughter-in-love) first Mother's Day. Unfortunately because of the mandates that were in place due to the pandemic, this special day was one of the first Mother's Days that Whitney would not get to spend with her own mother. While I was thinking about what I could do for Tarsha, she was thinking about what she could do for Whitney. So, Tarsha called and asked her if they would like to come over for dinner, and they accepted the invitation. Tarsha cooked some delicious smothered chicken at Whitney's request, and man was it delicious along with the entire menu of other items that could have fed a small village! As I watched her prepare for that day, at no time did she give thought to why she should be the one being served; she simply served. It is that sort of thoughtfulness for the well-being of others that makes her such a beautiful person to me. I thank God that He has blessed me with a wife that is not only beautiful on the outside, but beautiful through and through. Take some time to investigate the lovely person your spouse is on the inside and you will be amazed at just how beautiful they are.

3. *Strong marriages require a willingness to share in the interests of your spouse even if those things are of no interest to you.*

Part of the mystery of romance and relationship is discovering the things that are unique about your spouse and sharing in those things.

Marriage requires compromise and accommodation when it comes to learning how to share interests that are not common to both people.

My favorite time of the year is football season. I love the game of football, and I especially enjoy college football. There is nothing like a full Saturday of great college football, however, Tarsha hasn't always shared my enthusiasm of sitting on the couch all day watching college football. One Saturday, she decided to try it out. In an effort to try to understand why I was so enthralled with collegiate sports, she sat down beside me quietly and just watched a game. That one game turned into two. That weekend turned into a string of weekends where she would watch multiple games with me while asking questions about the games themselves. What is that formation called? Why did the referee throw that flag? What is that position called? You get the picture.

That was then, this is now. I can't keep her away from the game, especially her Dallas Cowboys. Because she unselfishly took an interest in something that I enjoy, we have one more thing that we can enjoy together. As a matter of fact, we have set a goal to attend an NFL game in every stadium and we are committed to make it happen. This would never have been an option had Tarsha not taken the initiative to share in one of my interests.

Before I close this thought, please understand that this goes both ways. Both parties must put the effort into sharing the interests of their spouse, whatever it takes. For instance, I enjoy action movies. When it comes to movies and television, give me some action, or give me comedy. Either of the two will do. However, Tarsha enjoys drama. CSI, Good Girls, Law & Order, The Resident, among others. So when she began to ask me to watch some of her shows with her, I wanted to say "I'll pass on the drama." But how could I? As I committed to share in this interest of hers, I came to enjoy the shows as well, and now binge watching certain shows has become a pastime that we enjoy together. Try something that your spouse enjoys in the coming week. In the long run, you'll be glad you did.

4. *Strong marriages require a willingness to respect the fact that occasionally your spouse needs some time away from you.*

Don't fool yourself, you need to spend some time alone. In our constantly connected world, being alone is often equated to people who are sad, lonely, introverted, or uncomfortable socializing. The truth is psychologists have discovered many benefits of spending time alone. Spending time alone allows you to: unwind, increase productivity and improve concentration. It provides the space to discover or rediscover yourself, and you can appreciate your relationships more after you have spent some quality time alone. Neither you or your spouse should feel guilty about the desire to spend time alone.

I have found that in the majority of couples that I have counseled, the woman usually is the one who feels guilty about spending time alone. She often feels obligated to take care of everyone else and as a result, often neglects her own self-care. Let me encourage you with this: Never feel guilty about spending time alone, for spending time alone is a form of self-care. Husband, help your wife take care of herself in this area. Spending time alone contributes to greater happiness, peace of mind and reduced stress, which all contribute to your wife being better able to do the things that fulfill her.

Even the closest friends need some time to be alone with their thoughts and those interests in which the other person chooses not to share at all. Tarsha enjoys occasionally talking on the phone with family and friends around the country for long periods of time. She knows I don't, so when she is engaged in this, I make sure that I am out of sight, and out of mind so she can enjoy that time free from attending to me and worrying if she has been on the phone too long. I enjoy taking long bubble baths and bike rides. When I am about to engage in one or the other, she gives me that space to be by myself hassle free. Don't take it personally, your spouse needs some time away from you. Give it to them with gladness.

Are you and your spouse best friends? Are you and your spouse content to be alone with each other? Do you and your spouse value one another for who you are on the inside, and not just how the other looks on the outside? Is there a willingness in you and your spouse to share in the interests of the other even if those things are of no interest to you? Do you and your spouse respect the fact that occasionally you each need time away from the other? If you answered yes to all five questions, then your marriage is a walking hashtag of what a strong marriage looks like. Take pride and handle it responsibly because someone needs to witness it so that they too can begin to experience a strong marriage.

Think About This:

Considering the four things that are listed in this chapter that help to identify a strong marriage, how many of the four do you feel are demonstrated in your marriage?

Write About This:

1. At the beginning of the chapter there is a summary of 4 things that Solomon offers as benefits of friendship. How many supporting examples of those statements can you give from your marriage?

Your answer can be as simple as something like *"We assembled a tent much faster when the two of us worked together rather than one person trying to do it alone. This is an example supporting the statement in #1– 'Two can work better than one.'"*

_____

_____

_____

_____

2. Set a timer for 5 minutes. Brag on your spouse for as much of that time as you can. Write everything you can think of that you love about them.

_____

_____

_____

_____

_____

_____

_____

3. Parents and teachers have been advised to praise publicly and reprimand privately. In the marital relationship we should follow the same rule. What are your thoughts on publicly praising your spouse?

_____

_____

_____

_____

_____

_____

4. Are there pros and cons to publicly praising your spouse? Explain your answer.

_____

_____

_____

_____

Have Fun With This:

"*Strong marriages involve couples who are content to be alone with each other.*" One childhood game we would play (albeit a very silly one) was seeing who could make the other person make a sound first. Try this out with your spouse. Sit facing each other and make sure the room is free from all noises. Stare at each other and see who lasts the longest without making any sound at all. What does this say about your marital relationship? Well...actually, it says nothing other than you are willing to do something different at the risk of making yourself look silly and just HAVING FUN!

Your Mama and Daddy Had Sex

SEXUAL INTERCOURSE HAS BEEN AND STILL IS A TOPIC that even married adults have difficulty discussing with each other so to discuss it with others is even more uncomfortable for most. By the moral standards of many, it is at the point of marriage that sex can be engaged in in a "guilt free manner." I could only giggle and drop my head in amusement (and a bit of embarrassment) when at his wedding reception, Cameron, our oldest son approached me and declared that "tonight I'm gonna have sex, sex, sex, sex." (The embarrassment was mainly from the fact that he was expressing this in front of 5 or 6 of his other 25 year old friends who I still viewed -as I viewed him- as these sweet little kids that used to be outside running around and playing ball). As I later thought about that brief conversation, I remembered a single line in a sermon by Louis Greenup where he explained one of the reasons that the men at this particular conference should not be ashamed of talking about sex in a Christian environment. He flat-footedly exclaimed and screamed at the top of his voice, "your mama and daddy had sex!" This is true for most of us. Right? So we can continue in the embarrassment of not discussing sex and intimacy because it is uncomfortable— or we can talk about the issues related to it and hopefully begin to reduce the percentage of marriages ending in divorce because of lack of satisfaction in the bedroom.

A couple years into our marriage, I realized that what was once a very enjoyable time together had now become more of a required chore that had to be done. Why? Because I thought of sex as something that my husband needed and something that I had to give him no matter how tired I was (and trust me I was tired 6 of the 7 nights a week). What I would find out a few years after that timeframe would change the sex game totally for us. Call me a slow learner or whatever you like, but it literally took at least 5 years or so for me to finally learn something that I will now share with you, the reader. Brace yourself for this...Sex is not just for nighttime! What a revolutionary idea. You mean, we could actually have sex in the daytime? Yep! No longer did every intimate interaction have to be after the children went to bed and then happen in such a quiet and restricted manner so as not to wake them up or keep them from discovering that their "mama and daddy had sex." No longer did my husband have to get the "sleepy sex" as he called it. And no longer did I have to run to the shower and pray for the energy to be supernaturally infused in me from on high so that I could please my husband (more to come on this prayer!)

By embracing the notion that sex was not just for nighttime, we turned on the parts of ourselves that had once caused us to giggle when we saw each other, our stomachs to have knots in them, and our hearts to leap because we knew the feelings that awaited at the end of the anticipation period. At that time, we both had jobs that were highly demanding but provided a great deal of flexibility in the hours worked. The first time he got the call to, "Meet me at home after your next appointment," any person seeing him re-enter his car to head to the next appointment probably wondered what had led to the new bounce in his step! We had learned the concept of working with the time we had and not allowing our sex life continually to diminish because we were too tired at night to devote the necessary time and attention to meeting the sexual needs of our mate.

There are many marriages that do not have the luxury of mid-day rendezvous but still have the issues of one of the two being overly tired or unable to consistently give his or her best efforts when it comes to sexual intimacy. This has been the case on numerous occasions in our marriage. I have shared with other wives and some couples as well that my bathroom and in particular my shower is one of the most sanctified places in my home. It is there where I have often gone to God at midnight, one o'clock, or two o'clock in the morning because my husband has turned over and whispered his famous come-on line of, "Hey, are you sleepy?" Early in the marriage, I would most often choose to answer through my silence and stiffened body, but as I matured, I chose to (as often as possible) see what I could do to meet him where he was at the moment. After that question was whispered in the midnight hour, I learned to remain silent and make my way through the darkness of the bedroom and into the bathroom, where I would whisper my own question. My question, however, would be directed to the God of my strength, simply something like, "Lord, I am very tired, and honestly, I am not really interested in having sex right now. Would You please give me the strength, the energy, and the desire needed to please my husband right now?" Without exception, I have been able to slip right back into bed shortly thereafter and connect with my husband for a time that was mutually satisfying to the both of us.

If yours is a relationship where one of the parties is never interested in being sexually intimate but the other one is, there are remedies available and strategies that can be explored so that this is not an issue of contention or a possible pathway to infidelity or divorce. Many marriage and family therapists specialize in working with couples and individuals to address such common situations. There are also solutions available through primary care physicians as well as gynecologists. The key is that whether you are addressing it as I have in the past or consulting with medical professionals, do not let different energy or interest levels in romantic encounters be a reason for the bedroom to become a despised place in your marriage. It should be the place where each person knows that he or she can express needs, fulfill needs and receive fulfillment as well.

Some of you may have quickly glossed over a phrase I used earlier in this chapter. I am referring to sex being a need for my husband. I remember when I was first exposed to this notion. It was during a presentation by the wife of a former pastor that we had. I wrestled with this when she first said it and hypothesized that she was likely a victim of the manipulation of a man whose hormones were uncontrollable. I listened a little while, but honestly unenthusiastically, to her likening the males need for sex to the need that many women have for conversation. It was definitely going to take more than a 45-minute workshop to convince me that my husband's sexual desire was an actual need. What I left the session with was not a full-blown convinced mindset that he legitimately needed sex, but rather a curiosity that would propel me to at least conduct my own (albeit unscientific) experimental research.

What I found was without being in any manner approached by me for sex, there was a predictable number of days that would pass, almost to the hour, before he would express a desire to be intimate. This was very much similar to a predictable inner clock of sorts that I have as it relates to eating or drinking. There is a set number of hours before my body initiates signs that it is ready to consume something again. Now, unlike eating or drinking and our need to satisfy our bodies with food or water, a man will not die if he does not have sex. Really men, you won't! I promise. However similarly to the physiological need we have for food and the accompanying regular signs for the same, the man experiences and often demonstrates those need-based signals. A number of books and scholarly articles have been written on the topic and would likely prove beneficial for those skeptics who are like I was when I was first introduced to the idea of sex being a need. Juli Slattery writes in her book No More Headaches, that

> a husband's _sexual desire_ is impacted by what's around him but is determined by biological factors, specifically the presence of testosterone in his body. Immediately after sexual release, men are physically satisfied. But as their sexual clock ticks on, sexual thoughts become more prevalent, and they are more easily aroused. The physical need for sexual release intensifies as sperm builds in the testicles. The body continues to produce and store sperm, although sperm production fluctuates based on levels of testosterone and the frequency of sexual release. The best way for a woman to understand this dynamic is to relate it to another physiological need. If you've had a baby, you may relate to the experience of milk building up in your breasts a few days after giving birth. The buildup of breast milk becomes annoying (and even painful) until the milk is expressed. You may have even

had the embarrassing experience of leaking breast milk when it was not expressed. A male's semen buildup is sometimes released through nocturnal emissions if it is not otherwise relieved. Just as with breast milk, sperm production tends to "keep up with demand." The more often a man has sex, the more semen his body is likely to produce.[10]

Once I continued to conduct my own experiments, expose myself to the research of medical professionals and read books that addressed the differences between the male and female psychological and physiological needs, I was better able to express my own needs and better able to anticipate and meet the needs and desires of my husband.

If my own experiments and the resources I consulted were not enough, the interaction described below and his actions that accompanied it definitely showed that if sex with me was not an actual need, it was certainly a strong desire that had one of the top priorities in his life. After several months of my coming to bed exhausted at minimum 5 nights a week, we had a heart-to-heart conversation about our sex life. I explained to Walter what he already knew: we had 2 small children, I had a very demanding job which took me away from the home at least 50 hours a week, and there was no shortage of laundry to be done, toilets to be cleaned, floors to be mopped, lunches to be packed and meals to be cooked. He looked at me intently and stated in no uncertain terms that he would prefer sandwiches and salads with good sex as opposed to no sex or tired sex with hot meals every day. Additionally he said that he would make greater efforts to help with the household chores so that the energy I once used for those things could be transferred to energetic efforts in the bedroom. After thinking about that for a few

---

[10] Slattery, J. (2009). No More Headaches: Enjoying Sex and Intimacy in Marriage. Carol Stream, IL: Tyndale House Publishers

minutes longer, (I imagine he started looking around at the disarray the house was in at the moment), he amended that to offer giving up some of our "miscellaneous" expenses and instead use those funds to have a housekeeper come in twice a month to assist with chores. What a wonderful idea for him to reallocate funds so that I could reallocate energy! From that point on, we have experienced the fullness associated with healthy and vibrant communication about sexual intimacy. I understand that his priorities are not *who* cleans or *what* is cooked but rather which version of his wife shows up in the bedroom.

Don't let sex be a taboo subject in your marriage. Not only should you not be reluctant to talk about it, a good idea is for you to check in regularly with each other to see how things are going. As mentioned in one of the first chapters, we were twenty years in before one of us made the statement, "I am realizing that we have different expectations when it comes to sex." I (Tarsha) was comfortable making the statement because we both understand that no topic, not even sexual intimacy, is off limits when we are talking about ways to improve our marriage and provide a more enjoyable atmosphere for each other. (If you are interested in how that conversation proceeded from there and the results, just remember to ask us to elaborate when you see us at a marriage conference and ...if you remember and are bold enough to ask, we will gladly answer!)

If you would feel uncomfortable right now putting down the book and telling your spouse something you enjoy about your intimate times together as well as something that you think could be improved on, you might consider ways in which you can work to overcome this discomfort. One great way is for each of you to consider whether you agree that sexual intimacy in the confines of a marriage is not only accepted in the Bible but it is encouraged. I Corinthians 7:3-5 lets us know that in a marital relationship, each person's body belongs to the other person, that neither has authority over their own body and that they should never deprive one another except for a limited agreed upon time to be devoted for praying. If either spouse disagrees with this, it is a spiritual issue rather than a sex issue and perhaps a spiritual mentor should be consulted. If this concept— that the Bible encourages healthy sexual relations within a marriage— is embraced by both the husband and the wife, then seek ways today to increase the levels of intimacy in your marital relationship. A great first step is to talk to one another about your sexual needs, the current frequency and level of sexual fulfillment in the relationship and how this can be an area that goes to great if it is already good or how it can improve if one or both of you feel that sexual intimacy is an area of dissatisfaction. Whatever the case, don't be afraid to talk about sex and in fact, take a break and talk about it now, don't be ashamed or embarrassed because after all...your mama and daddy had sex!

Think About This:

Are there things about your sex life that you are uncomfortable discussing with your spouse?

Write About This:

1. Think about the average person's ideas related to sexual intimacy in marriage. Their ideas could revolve around things like: the frequency, the time of day, who should initiate, foreplay and/or after play expectations and even things like whether the lights should be on or off or whether there needs to be lingerie worn or not. The list goes on and on for what people expect in the area of sexual intimacy

in the context of marriage. What are some of the expectations regarding sexual intimacy that you had coming into the marriage that were different than the expectations that your spouse had?

_____

2. What are some of the expectations that were the same for both of you?

_____

_____

_____

_____

_____

3. Were the differences in expectations ever talked about? If so, explain. If not, why weren't they?

_____

_____

_____

_____

4. Have they been resolved?

_____

_____

_____

_____

_____

5. If so, how did the resolution come about? If not, what steps can you take to move toward discussing and determining whether the expectations should be or can be met?

_____

_____

_____

_____

_____

Have Fun With This:

Be creative, have fun and come up with your own activity for this section!

WHAT HAPPENED TO MY BANANA?

WE OFTEN COMMENT TO PEOPLE THAT IT SEEMS LIKE WE were taken through an early, intensive and accelerated course in the cycles, seasons, stages (you take your pick of words) of marriage. What I mean by that is that in the first 4 years or so, we experienced several lengthy spans of time where we got along well— we had healthy life/work/family balance and we were doing OK financially and intimately. Also during those 4 years, we experienced spans of time where we were barely surviving in those same areas just mentioned. There were times in those first few years that we were the ones giving advice to other couples about how to cultivate an environment for a loving, healthy home and there were times where we felt we did not have a clue about what it would take to get ourselves out of the pit of daily despair that both of us agreed we were in. We now recognize that the timing during which we experienced our most intense marital challenges could not have been better for us. It was a time when our children were young enough that they were pretty much oblivious to how unhappy we were. Also as we consider the roles that each of us would later need to play in our chosen occupations, ministry and positions in the community, we know that our ability to effectively function in those roles while dealing with marital conflict would have resulted in our hurting others outside of just ourselves.

One day as I was putting away groceries, I found myself thinking about how many couples I knew who seemed to make it through decades of marriage and for reasons often not fully understood by even themselves, decided to call it quits. The people that came to my mind were couples that were actual mentors to other couples and seemed to be at that stage in marriage where they were best friends and sailing smoothly through life. The timing of my thoughts appeared odd to me given that I was simply taking the bananas out the bag. It was then that I really went into deep thought about not only the marriages of these type couples but also I began reflecting on where we were in our marriage having been empty nesters for just over a year or so.

I really enjoy bananas. A banana is most appealing to me when it has just turned from green to yellow and only partially about to get the brown and black hues. Not too hard and not too gooey is what I consider the perfect banana. If I buy the banana just like that from the store, I would need to consume it right away. Understanding that in general I am buying the bananas to eat later throughout the week, I intentionally purchase the pale green bananas from the store so that I have a couple days' worth of great bananas as they turn from green to yellow. The bananas are so delicious to me when they are "just right". Not many days after that "just right stage," my perfect banana begins to turn brown and it gets extremely soft and in fact, I really want to either throw it away or sometimes mix it with other ingredients and enjoy it in a smoothie. My preference is to eat the banana without anything else. As it ages, however, I may begin to use it in other ways that still bring satisfaction to my appetite- a fruit smoothie or banana bread. The week-old banana's texture and appearance does not surprise me because I expected it to become that way. In our marriages, we should expect that over time, physical appearances along with a number of other characteristics of our spouse will change.

In marriages, over time, we may enjoy certain things about our relationships such as training for marathons or travelling the world, but as time goes on, things you enjoy may be less physical but still as enjoyable. The expected changes are manageable but sometimes initially challenging. What about times when the good banana, not over a matter of days, but quite suddenly turns brown with no real warning? I have taken with me a perfect banana as I left the house and within minutes sometimes because of its exposure to direct sunlight or an extreme temperature change or even just being slightly punctured at one end or another, my perfect banana turns into the banana that I really just want to throw away. How could something so perfect go bad that quickly?

There are times when couples seem to have crossed into what seems like a perfect season of marriage, maybe it is just as the last child has moved out of the home, or maybe it is when the couple finds that they are finally debt free. Maybe it is when both spouses have finally settled into true retirement and are no longer concerned about the daily duties that most people have to balance with their home life. The husband and wife are really liking and loving one another and seemingly have entered a stage very similar to dating where they have eyes only for each other and the majority of their waking hours includes some aspect of their spouse. The ease at which they communicate, the effort-less automatic recognition of the other person's needs, and the desire to spend time with one another produces a joy and a peace that was worth all the time and energy that finally got them to this stage of marriage. Euphoria in every sense of the word is where this couple is. Suddenly out of nowhere, like my banana which changed in a matter of moments not days, the euphoria of this marriage switches to distress. Conditions changed in the marital atmosphere. Sometimes it can be as simple as a question asked at the wrong time. Maybe it was a request by another family member for something to be done. Perhaps it was just a week where energy levels were down and stress levels were up for one or both spouses.

As mentioned more than once in this book, the early years of our marriage had so many arguments, fights, silent times and questions of "is this really going to work?" As the years went by however and it seemed like our relationship was looking like my perfect banana, the peaceful and joyful times became the norm for us rather than the exception. We expected to have evenings filled with laughter, an auto-matic desire to please the other, spending time together and genuinely enjoying doing things that the other person suggested. We were at a season in our marriage where the nest was now empty, we had a good grasp on our finances, our children were doing well, our careers were stable and when we were physically apart from each other, at the fore-front of our minds was how soon we would be able to reunite.

The only problem was that because these stretches of euphoria were lasting so long and had become the normal way of life for us, whenever there was any inkling that there was about to be a disagreement, we did not want to confront it or when it was confronted, it often went unre-solved because of our subconscious desire to return quickly to euphoria.

We were, in a way, afraid that our "great marriage" would somehow be placed on some slippery slope to marital destruction. Our *good* place was no longer a *safe* place. It was not a safe place for each person to voice their disagreement on a topic. Heaven forbid that we get into an argument and it ends up with us not talking for three days. We shuttered at the thought of the other person's feelings being hurt and that resulting in a whole night filled with a cloud of disappointment in the house. When difficult or potentially contentious issues had to be addressed, as seasoned as we were in marriage, we would often avoid the topics or prematurely end the discussion.

Eventually, we had to commit to reminding each other that when the challenging situations arise, our wonderful relationship is not any less wonderful just because we disagreed. This may be where you are in your marriage. The point where your relationship is just like the perfect banana but you look around and literally out of nowhere, the banana appears ready to be thrown out. During these times remind yourself that it is ok to have "spirited conversations." It is just fine to admit when you are not feeling up to what the other person has suggested you would be doing that day. It is perfectly acceptable to question why your spouse said or did something that you did not understand. We had to remember that these times of healthy communication that allowed opportunities for the exchange of different ideas were spaces to *grow* rather than spaces to *avoid*. The sign of a healthy relationship is not the absence of difficult times. A healthy marriage is demonstrated by a husband and wife who can recognize issues, identify solutions and navigate through them back to a time of peace and harmony. Enjoy, appreciate and bask in the times where you are void of major problems in your relationship. Times when the money is good, the intimacy is great and the time spent with each other is simply indescribable. During those times when the occasional issues pop up-- and they will-- embrace them as opportunities to step up and be more loving, quicker to forgive and to show more patience than you would have in the past. As with life, our challenging times are those times that we look back on and realize that it was then when we built muscle, stamina and inner strength.

Think About This:

The author discusses times when an issue can go unresolved because spouses do not want to address the issue during a time where things are otherwise pretty calm and peaceful? What are some benefits and what are some dangers of handling issues in this manner? Can you think of a time in your relationship when you chose to avoid an important issue because you felt that discussing it had the potential of "rocking the boat" which had been relatively steady at that point?

Write about This:

1. When it comes to responding to change, some people are:

    •   non-reactive (they won't respond in hopes that things will just go back to the way they were)

    •   immediately reactive (Often responding —I have to do something... anything...and I have to do it now)

    •   willing to embrace it and accept it in a positive way as just a part of life (evaluating it based upon past experiences, resources available, benefits and consequences, and determining the best course of action)

Which is your usual response to a change that you don't like? If you cannot identify yourself in either, think of a recent experience where a negative change was in front of you. Describe the experience and describe how you responded or are currently responding to it.

_____

_____

_____

_____

_____

_____

2. Describe the last major change that you and your spouse experienced in your relationship?

_____

_____

_____

_____

_____

_____

Have Fun With This:

Things change; people change. Look at two pictures of yourself, one from recently and another from your childhood or from as far back as you can. Referencing the pic from the distant past, describe for your spouse how people would have described your inner characteristics, attitudes, tendencies and personality traits. Give examples as much as possible. In what ways, if any, have you changed.

A Few Marital Nuggets

THE FOLLOWING NUGGETS ARE THINGS THAT MAY HAVE been mentioned earlier in the book but most of them were not. In no particular order, we offer to you these nuggets to think about and to apply.

1. You have to give your spouse the right to complain without taking it personally and getting upset. This builds trust when they know they can share how they feel without negative repercussions.

2. Appreciation is the oil that lubricates any relationship. Without it, the gears get stuck. Use descriptive praise. Be specific in your praise of your spouse. Praise your spouse 10 times as much as you complain or criticize.

3. Adopt a teachable spirit. Without it, it's very difficult to get better at anything. Allow your spouse to teach you about the things he/she likes and dislikes. Remember, as seasons change, these things are likely to change and you want to assure you are up to date with your spouse's updates.

4. Make it a priority to read at least one book a year together on each of these topics: marriage, communication, finances, and intimacy. *If you have been through all the other chapters in this book, you are well on your way to completing this marital nugget!*

5. Bad friends and negative influences can wreak havoc on marriages. Divorce, addiction, and adultery run in packs. You'll find when these things are present, there's always some sort of support system for it. Disconnect from every support system that negatively influences your marriage.

6. Take the responsibility of helping to build your spouse's confidence. Be your spouse's biggest cheerleader.

7. Think about how much you planned for your wedding. Make sure that periodically you plan for the continued success of your marriage. Just as you put thought into what you wanted the day to be like, who you wanted to participate with you, where you wanted the wedding to be, whether you should enlist a wedding coordinator, what the wedding budget would be, make sure you strategically address these same aspects in your marriage. What is the atmosphere you want your marriage to reflect? Who should be involved with you to help you reach

those goals, who are people that can provide sound counsel? What is the "cost" for a successful marriage? Schedule regular planning sessions with your spouse to review, assess and plan for future success.

8. Give your spouse something to imitate. Think about how you want to be treated and then act that way. Better yet, think about how you want someone to treat your son or your daughter and then act that way. If your spouse imitated all of your behaviors, what type of marriage would you have?

9. Have at least 3 couples that you regularly interact with. Be sure that one is more experienced on the marital journey than you are; they can help guide the way. Find one who is less sea-soned than you are in marriage. By sharing words with them about your own successes and failures, your walk as a couple can be strengthened. Also, find a couple that is at a similar stage in marriage as you are. Companions on a journey tend to help make the trip more enjoyable because many times sim-ilar challenges and similar successes are occurring around the same times.

THINK, WRITE <u>and</u> HAVE FUN WITH THIS

If you were offered a prize that you could not refuse in exchange for honestly and thoroughly addressing, implementing, and practicing as necessary each aspect of all of the nuggets listed above, which of them would

- be the easiest for you to do?

- be the most difficult?

- have you thinking "oh well, never mind, I'll pass on the prize"?

_____

_____

_____

_____

_____

_____

_____

_____

_____

_____

Concluding Thoughts

CONGRATULATIONS ON INVESTING THE TIME AND effort needed to complete this book! We have prayed God's blessings for every person that picks up this God-inspired work. We sincerely hope that with this book, we have played a role in helping to strengthen your relationship with your spouse or significant other. We are firm believers that solid marriages lead to more stable communities and these communities ultimately will allow for stronger societies all over the globe. Continue working hard to build the stamina required to not only survive in your marriage but to truly thrive. We would be honored to be your workout partners! Let us journey with you individually, as a couple or with groups that you may be a part of. We have many years of experience counseling individuals and couples as well as serving as Conference Presenters and Conference Planners. If you would like to consider us for your next event or get more information on other services we provide, check out our website at www.waltergibsonministries.com

Walter and Tarsha Gibson